Sex, Sleep or Scrabble?

To everyone
who put a hand up

· · · · · · · · · · ·

'The real voyage of discovery consists not in seeking new
landscapes but in having new eyes.'
Marcel Proust *(author)*

· · · · · · · · · · · · ·

'Life. Be in it.'
Brian Dixon *(Australian Rules footballer)*

· ·

'First do no harm.
Next give some pleasure.'
Dr Phil *(modified hedonist)*

· · · · · · · · · · · · · · ·

Also by Dr Phil

Medicine Balls

Trust Me, I'm (Still) a Doctor

Coming Soon:
The Rude Health Show (DVD)

For more info:
www.drphil2.com

Sex, Sleep or Scrabble?

Seriously funny answers to life's quirkiest queries

Dr Phil Hammond

BLACK & WHITE PUBLISHING

First published 2009
by Black & White Publishing Ltd
29 Ocean Drive, Edinburgh EH6 6JL

1 3 5 7 9 10 8 6 4 2   09 10 11 12 13

ISBN: 978 1 84502 271 6

A CIP catalogue record for this book is available from the British Library.

Typeset by Ellipsis Books Limited, Glasgow
Printed and bound by MPG Books Limited, Bodmin

Contents

Contents

Contents

Contents

Contents

Introduction

. . . .

'Sex, Sleep or Scrabble?'

It's ten o'clock at night, the kids have finally pretended to go to sleep and supper has worked its way through the top half of your gut. So what do you fancy? Sex, sleep or Scrabble? When I ask an audience for a show of hands, it splits neatly into thirds. When I ask for a show of opinion, it gets far more complicated. Apparently, you don't need to be over fifty to enjoy Scrabble. And you can combine it with sex, either before — a bit of stiff intellectual competition makes fine foreplay — or after, if you don't smoke. Or you can play Sex Scrabble, where every word drips with moist, purple innuendo (and you seldom make it past the opening round).

Most people find it hard to resist rude words in word games. In *Countdown*'s Dictionary Corner next to the delightful Susie Dent, I once had a 'woody' and a 'boner' in the same game. On reflection, I think the boner was Susie's, but I stole it from her. We had to stop recording for several minutes for the giggling to die down. Des Lynam held it all together like a consummate professional, but left the show shortly afterwards. I still worry that Susie's boner did for him.

For some, expanding 'end' into 'innuendo' for a triple-word score is hell on earth. Being forced to play board games with crustaceous relatives at Christmas can leave you scarred for life, but all couples should at least try a game of pre-marital Scrabble before tying the knot. If your partner doesn't take it terribly seriously, allows you to graze the dictionary for inspiration and is happy to abandon the game when you've fallen asleep, then he (or she) is likely to be equally laid-back to live with. If he only plays competition rules, criticizes your spelling and limited vocabulary, insists on seeing it out until the bitter end and takes a copy of the score sheet up to the bedroom to taunt you with, then at least you've been warned.

Scrabble, like Monopoly, Risk and other wholesome family games, can easily turn into an instrument of torture in the wrong hands. It's a deceptively small leap from the game-board to the water-board. Anyone who boasts repeatedly about his winning 'manihoc' or highlights your absurdly naive tactics in front of his mates is probably not going to be very helpful during childbirth or when your mother gets dementia. If you want to know what your future holds together, have plenty of Scrabble before marriage.

After marriage, sleep tends to be the most popular ten o'clock option, at least for mothers. It's an unfortunate evolutionary quirk that men often want sex when women most want to sleep, and there's no easy solution. If you opt for sleep, the man rolls around complaining that he can't kip on a stiffy or tries to have a sly tug that registers on the Richter scale. Wake up, lend him a hand and get it over quickly. If you opt for tired sex, you also want it done and dusted in under a hundred strokes, so you need to stop thinking about tomorrow's shopping or what's happening in *The Wire*, and make a few of those ridiculous noises that always get him going.

On no account try to solve the sex-sleep dilemma with the compromise of knackered Scrabble. You won't spot his cheeky 'flange' and you'll be too tired to come up with anything more taxing than 'bed', leaving you wide open to ridicule. And if you're a light sleeper, there's nothing worse than being woken by that 4am rollover onto the missing 'P'.

Just like the game, the Scrabble debate at my shows goes on and on, at least for those who manage to stay awake. But when it comes to audience questions, nearly all of them are about sex, or the things that happen to your body that stop you enjoying it. There's far more pleasure to be had in life than ninety seconds of hide the sausage, but it still dominates our hang ups (and hang downs). So it is with this book. As a half-Australian comedy doctor, I'm immune to rudery, though some of you may prefer Scrabble to Forbidden Fruits. But if you stick with it you'll discover words you only dreamt of.

Dr Phil

September 2009

1

Not so simple pleasures

Most of us spend our lives trying to balance pleasure and harm, so it's odd that the only medical lecture I've attended that even mentioned the 'P' word was about sticking an electrode into a rat's brain. In doing this, a Canadian researcher called James Olds stumbled on a part of the brain entirely devoted to pleasure. When the electrode was attached to a pedal, the rat would press it thousands of times an hour for maximum pleasure. A bit like a teenage boy and his penis.

That was back in 1954, and teenage rats and boys have been peddling furiously ever since. But pleasure has never really taken off as a serious subject for doctors. Type it into the search engine of the mighty National Institute for Health and Clinical Excellence (www.nice.org.uk) and it returns not a single hit. Pleasure gets just two mentions in the *Oxford Textbook of Medicine* (in relation to condom usage and physiotherapy), whereas stress weighs in with one hundred and twenty-seven. As with our news media, it seems medicine is obsessed with frightening us into compliance and accentuating the negative rather than helping people to be happy.

Doctors very rarely tell patients to pleasure themselves (for fear of getting struck off), but anything above a rodent is hardwired to seek it out. The Japanese call enjoyment 'Tanoshimi'. What little research that has been done suggests a regular dose of pleasure strengthens your immune system and keeps both mind and body healthy by relieving stress. And it's cheap. If you close your eyes and think of the things you really enjoy, most don't cost much.

Enjoyment is a personal thing, but the concept is not new. Alcohol has been invented and used in every known culture, especially those in which it is banned. Stories, sex, siestas, chocolate, pets, dancing, laughter, cakes and coffee are just as ubiquitous – although not necessarily in that order. It seems there is a basic human need for us to enjoy ourselves and, if you believe Charles Darwin, there must be some evolutionary advantage in hedonism, provided you keep it under control. The trick is to enjoy life without harming yourself or those around and inside you.

But pleasure doesn't last long if you ruin it with regret. One study found that some women feel more guilty about eating ice cream than committing adultery. And committing adultery with ice cream is what keeps therapists in business.

Humans are social animals and pleasure generally requires some form of connection – to friends, family, fantasy, food, art or the environment. But to connect takes time and although we seem to have more of everything else than we had sixty years ago (money, possessions, sexually transmitted infections) we have less time to enjoy them (or at least put a condom on properly).

Very few pleasures aren't improved by slowing down (except perhaps running from bulls). Going slow allows you to connect more, consume less and remember enough to make a story out of it. Stories allow us to recycle pleasure constantly. They last forever, reinvent themselves and give us surprises, meanings and metaphors for life. And if you can enjoy your own story, as well as the stories of others, you're more resilient when shit happens, and more able to pass your story on.

I'm a big fan of skinny-dipping in the summer. Let the budgie breathe. After fifty lengths, it looks as if it's taken off. I don't do it in the winter for fear he'll never return to the perch. I used to do it in the sea but nudist beaches are on the wane owing to coastal erosion, so the joy of feeling the salty wind whistle through the lower regions may have to be put on hold. Still, it makes it a lot safer to squat in a rock pool (a sure way to get you shouting 'Tanoshimi', unless you enjoy the old-fashioned way of catching limpets).

If you slow down too much, don't you get pressure sores?

If you're having a day in bed, it's wise to roll over occasionally or shift from one buttock to the other to keep the circulation flowing. But slowing down doesn't (or needn't) equate with doing nothing. The slower I go, the more I think. I've perfected the art of slow exercise – moving just fast enough to be slightly breathless but never so fast as to be thoughtless or speechless. Most comedians find that idle thoughts are often their funniest.

The slow movement is nothing new. Life may not always have been sweet for a medieval peasant, but they had more public holidays and far fewer key performance indicators than us. During the Industrial Revolution, the work ethic was rammed home from the pulpit and you were made to feel guilty if you didn't enslave yourself to the production-line machine.

Time and energy are both limited, and if we burn too much up chasing dull, repetitive, unrewarding targets, the only escape is to try to squeeze in some instant gratification after work. So a bottle of wine or a six-pack of Stella disappears in half an hour and you have to do tomorrow's dull repetitive tasks with a jackhammer in your brain.

Some people manage to get pleasure from work, particularly if they don't do too much of it. As Tom Hodgkinson, founder and editor of the (twice-yearly) *Idler* magazine puts it:

> *A characteristic of the idler's work is that it looks suspiciously like play. This makes the non-idler feel uncomfortable. Victims of the Protestant work ethic would like all work to be unpleasant. They feel that work is a curse, that we must suffer on this earth to earn our place in the next. The idler, on the other hand, sees no reason not to use his brain to organise a life for himself where his play is his work, and so attempt to create his own little paradise in the here and now.*

Are we really less happy than we were in the fifties?

Hard to say. Comparing happiness in different eras is a bit like comparing sportsmen. Rod Laver or Roger Federer, Ronaldo or Eusebio, Geoff Capes or Hercules? How can you make a comparison when the hair was so different?

At least with sporting achievement, you can define what you want to measure but happiness is both harder to get a handle on and easier to interfere with. Telling Roger he wasn't as great as Rod probably won't affect him much, but the steady drip of psychologists telling us we're not happy anymore could talk us into a global depression. Or at least it might if they didn't have a twelve-step plan to dig us out again.

Just about everyone I see (and work with) has a rumbling, low-grade anxiety going on in the background of their lives. Sometimes it breaks through and the jitters take over for a while, but for most of us it just sits there, gnawing away at bits of the brain we didn't know existed (like the hippocampus), wearing us down and paving the way for depression.

The causes of this anxiety can be knocked up quickly by any Professor of Common Sense at the University of the Blindingly Obvious. Debt, time-pressure, bullying, entrapment, loss of control, worrying about the kids, media-induced fear, politically-induced fear, advertising-induced envy, a lack of meaning and purpose, uncertainty, isolation and insecurity. Doctors get very anxious having to deal with all this in less than ten minutes, along with hitting the cholesterol and diabetes targets (and dealing with our own doubts).

My wise GP trainer used to say: 'Life is a pool of shit and our job is to direct people to the shallow end.' I see it more as bodies floating down a river. As a doctor, you get so knackered pulling them out and putting them back together again, that no one has time to wander upstream and stop them jumping in.

The idler's approach is to camp out on the bank and watch the bodies floating past. You downsize, you live as cheaply (and consume as little) as you can and you make your own entertainment where you live. As Samuel Johnson put it: 'the wise idler will allow events and goods to come to him rather than expend energy and money travelling to disenchanting locations.'

Slowing down also gives you more time to listen to music, and the most concise advice on happiness comes from songs. I once waded through 600 pages of a book on how to keep yourself sane to discover it all came down to 'Ac-Cent-Tchu-Ate the Positive, E-Lim-In-Ate the Negative', written by Johnny Mercer for Bing Crosby and the Andrews Sisters in 1944. And one of the best self-help country classics to come out of the fifties was 'A

9

Satisfied Mind' by Red Hayes and Jack Rhodes. It includes such wisdom as:

> *How many times have you heard someone say*
> *'If I had his money, I could do things my way?'*
> *Little they know that it's so hard to find*
> *One rich man in ten with a satisfied mind.*

and

> *Money can't buy back your youth when you're old*
> *Or a friend when you're lonely, or a love that's*
>   *grown cold*
> *The wealthiest person is a pauper of a kind*
> *Compared to the man with a satisfied mind.*

The song was a No.1 for Porty Wagoner in 1955, and has been covered by Johnny Cash (on the *Kill Bill Vol 2* soundtrack) and Jeff Buckley (if you like posthumous poignancy). Bob Dylan murders it on *Saved* but my favourite version is by Jonathan Richman on the album *Jonathan Goes Country*. Richman is something of a personal hero, not least for his infectious enthusiasm. He once performed with 'I love life' on his t-shirt. My favourite obscure country band, the Ozark Mountain Daredevils, also covered it. Their album *It'll shine when it shines* is an idlers' classic.

So there you have it. The secret of happiness is a satisfied mind. That's why we were happier in the fifties. A mind needs time and space to put its feet up on the bank and appreciate the wisdom of country music. So cut out the crap and clutter, and learn to say 'no' – particularly to happiness questionnaires.

NOTE: Idling is fine up to a point, but someone still has to clean the toilet; preferably the person who just idly pissed all over the seat. If you're going to slow down, there's no excuse for not improving your aim. As someone with English, Irish and Australian heritage, I've dribbled all over the world and concluded that the secret of life is to feel comfortable in your skin wherever you happen to be. Just peel it back first.

Comfortable in your own skin also means comfortable in your own company. If you can enjoy yourself on your own, it really doesn't matter if someone chucks you on Christmas Eve because your hair's too ginger and then runs off with your brother.

Is sex the greatest pleasure there is?

You decide. A lot more work has been done rating pain. Doctors often ask you to come up with a number between one and ten for hurt, and there's even a league table of painful events, with kidney stones jostling for top spot with childbirth, cruciate ligament tears and cluster headaches. But much less research has been done into pleasure, partly because we're obsessed with the negative but also because it's very hard to compare, say, the sweaty intensity of sex with the relaxed wonder of butterflies on the buddleia.

Pleasure needs plenty of variety. Think of it as food. If you draw a pie chart of your daily pleasure intake, it should have more than pies in it. Recreational sex is like a cream bun. Fine as a treat but you can't live off it. You need the protein of love and friendship and the slow-burning starch of broader passions. You can't compare masturbation with meditation. You need a bit of both.

Sex (solo or otherwise) at least has the capacity to provide very intense pleasure without causing any harm, which puts it streets ahead of any drug. And all for the price of a condom. But as with a drug, the drive for sex can stop you enjoying other pursuits. If you've got the itch, sex is everywhere you look, no matter how hard you try to divert it. Even butterflies. There are few more romantic sights than a pair of dancing Fritillaries. And why's that Purple Emperor lurking near the Painted Lady? Sex needs a sense of perspective. If it isn't available, sort yourself out and go and admire the Red Admirals. Man cannot live on instant gratification alone. And women find it even less gratifying.

Is happiness as contagious as swine flu?

No. But a study published in the *British Medical Journal* (in 2009) found that in any community, there are 'non-random clusters' of happy and miserable people i.e. happy people are more likely to be found living near each other than would occur by chance alone. And the same goes for miserable people. This could be because happy people cut all the miserable people out of their lives and surround themselves with other optimists. Or — as this study seems to suggest — happiness spreads across boundary walls. It also suggests that to be happy, you have to interact with others rather than keep it all to yourself. And to prove it, you have to fill in another bloody happiness questionnaire.

Everything we do is driven by our mood but — rather like sex — the British aren't too keen on talking about feelings. No one is happy all the time but those who manage a good percentage of happy days seem to be very adept at mood-flipping; getting yourself out of a miserable hole before it gets too deep. In a relationship, humour can be the best way of flipping your partner's mood (though it can backfire badly if you get the timing wrong). On your own, music is probably the quickest mood-flipper but you can't spend your entire life attached to an iPod because: a) you'll go deaf; and b) you'll have no friends. You need lots of variety on your pleasure plate.

Can you enjoy being miserable?

Not all the time. A persistent inability to find pleasure in anything, particularly in things that you used to enjoy, is a good indicator of depression. It's also a side effect of recreational drugs that burn up all the brain's pleasure chemicals in one instantly gratifying explosion, and then leave you absolutely floored and fucked and looking older than a scrotum.

Some people are born with a 'half-empty' rather than a 'half-full' default mood, and it takes more effort to flip between them into optimism. And a lot of people are just too stressed, busy or tired to have fun. But shit happens to all of us eventually, and it is possible to get and give pleasure in coming to terms with it. That's how comedians earn a living.

Relationships probably give people most pleasure and pain. As Kary Mullis put it, in his Biology Laureate Nobel Prize lecture in 1993: 'There is a general place in the brain, I think, reserved for the melancholy of relationships past. It grows as life progresses, forcing you finally, against your grain, to listen to country music.' If you're struggling with unrequited love and need a dose of melancholy, I'd prescribe 'He stopped loving her today' by George Jones.

A dog, a job and a knob. Do I need anything else?

A little food and water perhaps, and somewhere warm to shelter. But we actually need relatively little to be happy. We're social animals and we like company, but a dog is much easier to live with than a human. It gives you unconditional love, finds you amusing when you're drunk, doesn't mind mess, doesn't mind if you get its name wrong and even gets excited if you come home smelling of another dog. It won't wake you up at midnight and ask, 'If I died, would you get another dog?' Its parents never visit. It reduces your blood pressure and your cholesterol (by eating your food) and keeps you active and supple (as you bend over to pick up the poo). And, if you're too depressed to put your pants on in the morning, it'll lick your testicles. You don't get that with Prozac. Or marriage.

They do, sadly, get sick and die so expect to do some serious grieving. A friend had two dogs, one of which needed to be put down. She arranged a home death with a friendly vet, and she wrapped the dog in a blanket on the lawn, with a piece of chicken in its mouth to distract it from the injection. The family gathered, music was played, poems were read and tears were shed as the other dog appeared frantically at the window. They let her out to say goodbye and she dived under the blanket, paying her last respects, before emerging with the chicken. Dogs will be dogs, and not everyone should have one. Some people just don't get it. Others hate the smell, the shit and the saliva. And there's a strong correlation between cruelty to animals and cruelty to children.

A job, or at least a sense of purpose, is important for health but it helps if you enjoy it. Money is less important than having control over what you do and how you do it. Our best comedies are about entrapment. Basil Fawlty stuck between Cybil and Manuel, Blackadder between Queenie and Baldrick . . . they're going nowhere. David Brent in *The Office*, Alan Partridge and Keith in *Marion and Geoff* are all trapped, either denying or bemoaning the futility of it all as they get dumped on from all angles. If you're an employer, hire people who can do the job and give them the freedom to do it without 147 targets and 326 key performance indicators . . . unless you want to make a sitcom out of their misery.

Is dogging anything to do with dogs?

Cramped sex with random strangers in cars has its moments, particularly if you chance upon the gear stick (increasingly likely with smaller, eco-friendly models). Dogging outdoors is less restricted, with more chance of breathing space and nettle burn.

The name apparently derives not from the position but from the pretence, when discovered, of searching in the bushes for a lost dog. (**TIP**: Pull your pants up first or it won't sound quite so plausible when read out in court.)

Is it healthy to sleep with a pet?

Not if you're allergic to animal fur or the pet normally lives underwater. A surprising number of people sleep with their pets, particularly in-between marriages. They can fart, moult, snore, hog the duvet, spread flees and dribble as well as any man, and some are natural hunter-gatherers during the night, so expect the restless legs. On the plus side, they're warm, usually affectionate, damp at both ends and are generally happy to see you in the morning. And you can always compare dog breath.

What are the side effects of 'budgie smuggling'?

'Budgie smuggling' is Australian slang for wearing swimwear so tight that the outline of your genitals resembles a small parrot. It generally only applies to men. Wearing tight pants of any sort, particularly in a hot climate, may lessen your sperm count and increase your chances of a fungal infection under the testicles (athlete's crotch aka scrot rot). Other than that, the only side effect is aesthetic. Not everyone enjoys public protrusion and some parrots are smaller than others, especially after a bracing swim.

Budgie smuggling in its literal sense is generally applied to a visitor who sneaks a companion bird into prison for a lonely inmate. The most recent documented example was in Ireland's high security Portlaoise prison in 2007, when a woman is alleged to have concealed the family pet 'inside her'. Budgies are sociable, but not generally that sociable. Still, she must have trained it well because it got through undetected and was later found, fit and well, in her husband's cell.

Many prisons now openly encourage budgie buddies because of the health benefits of having something pretty to care for that won't answer back (budgies can mimic up to ten words but rarely construct the sort of sentence to send a prisoner over the edge). Check out the Sony-award-winning podcast *The Prisoner and the Budgerigar*. It tells the story of lonely Les, doing six years for violent crime in Bristol, and his relationship with Pig, his budgie. Les was able to 'get me a bird' not from inside his wife but from the budgie breeder on the inside. He haggled over the price, chose an egg and marked it with a pencil. 'I'd go down there with some of the other prisoners, and we'd check on how our eggs were coming along. We were fully grown men, worried about a batch of eggs, waiting for ours to crack. When mine did, I scooped him up and took him back to my cell to start his education.'

Pig was restless in his cage (probably coming to terms with his name) and his scratching and scuttling at night drove Les to distraction. So he took him to bed with him. 'At first I was worried I would squash him, but it never happened and he spent most nights sleeping with me.' Les likened looking after Pig to bringing up a baby: 'If I hadn't fed him, he would have died.' This new found responsibility seemed to help Les reflect on his life and make him want to be a more responsible person on his release. 'That bird did me good. Getting Pig was the best decision I ever made.'

If I was living in a cell, I'd be first in line for an egg. In fact, I'm thinking of starting up my own budgie therapy. I'll mate them in the waiting room and let the eggs pop out and hatch in full view. Anyone thinking of becoming a parent but not sure they're up to it could try a budgie first. If it's still alive after six months, they could swap it for a gerbil, then maybe a cat, gradually building up to a baby over a couple of years. I could also do a trial of budgie versus counselling for anyone miserable, lonely and tired of life. Obviously, you'd need to provide round-the-clock support for questions about cage size, faddy eating and bird fanciers' lung. But what is NHS Direct for? Budgies on prescription. You know it makes sense. Until bird flu returns.

Is it really good to touch the green, green grass of home?

Yes, if you're lucky enough to have any grass around your home. According to Natural England, 'access to green space' is diminishing year on year. Our parents and grandparents had far more to run about in than we do. Everyone needs a bit of green. It improves your mood, makes you feel less stressed, makes you recover more quickly from stressful situations and makes you want to get off your arse. Ask anyone over forty where their favourite childhood space was and it may well be up a tree. For many people under forty it'll be in front of a screen.

You don't just want to touch the grass either. Roll off into the long stuff. Look at the wildflowers and name the beetles. Put a blade between your thumbs and blow. Burn off each other's ticks. And don't forget your antihistamine. One study of American children found they could recognise a hundred corporate logos but not ten local flowers.

The song itself was written by Claud 'Curly' Putman Junior and recorded by (amongst others) Tom Jones, Elvis, Johnny Cash, John Otway (the funniest version) and Björn Ulvaeus's Hootenanny Singers. It's a cheesy, sting-in-the-tail country classic. A man is homeward bound, about to jump off the train and into the arms of his sweet Mary (with her 'hair of gold and lips like cherries') and then you realise he's daydreaming on death row with a sad old padre. The closest he'll come to climbing the old oak tree of his childhood is when they bury him beneath it. In recent versions, the old oak tree is replaced by the X-Box 3.

Is pulling your nose a polite way to masturbate in public?

Politer than going the whole hog, certainly. Men are more likely to pull a nose or ear in public than women. Some therapists say it's a substitute for masturbation, others claim it's a partial regression to thumb-sucking, a few say it's a mark of a liar. Some people pull the nose and squeeze the nostrils together because they enjoy the smell of the inside of the nose. The nasal glands are a poor substitute for smegma but better than nothing. Rubbing greasy hair against your scalp and sniffing will also get a few pheromones on your fingers.

Is swearing good for you?

There hasn't been much research into the health benefits of swearing except at Keele University, which suggests they've got too much bloody time on their hands. Sixty-four 'volunteers' were invited to put a hand in a tub of freezing water and keep it in there while repeating a swear word of their choice. Then they did it again while repeating 'a more commonplace, neutral word used to describe a table'. And guess what? When you swear, you can endure pain for fifty per cent longer (or an average of forty seconds).

Researcher Richard Stevens has several theories to explain this. The first is the competency theory – when you hit your head on a low lintel, you look like a skeletally-incompetent idiot, but swearing quickly reasserts your competency and control of the situation. Angry swearing also increases your heart rate and puts your body into fight mode, which in turn increases your pain tolerance (in case some bastard lintel hits you again).

My theory is that people (particularly men) can't multi-skill and if you ask them to think of 'a more commonplace, neutral word used to describe a table' it uses up all their powers of concentration and they can no longer fight the pain. I can't even think of one when I'm not in pain. Clearly, more studies are needed.

Dr Stevens also postulated that – like antibiotics – the over-use of swearing can negate its beneficial effects when you really need them because it no longer provokes the required emotional response. So you should swear sparingly. But swearing is far more versatile than just an angry, surprised response to pain. It can convey pleasure and love too. Just take the word 'fuck.' Derived from a Germanic verb meaning to move quickly (often far too quickly), and perhaps borrowed from the Middle Dutch *fokken* (to strike or copulate with). But now it's most often used in a non-sexual sense. It can be a transitive verb ('Tony fucked Gordon') or an intransitive verb ('Gordon was fucked by Tony'). It can be a noun ('Tony doesn't give a fuck about Gordon') or an adverb ('Gordon is fucking angry with Tony'). For more examples of deeply sensitive swearing, see *The Blair Years* by Alastair Campbell.

Do people in glasses get more passes?

No. They just spot the passes better with their glasses on. I did consider having my eyes lasered in the mid nineties, when the treatment first became popular, but all the eye surgeons I met still wore glasses, which put me off. They were waiting to see what the long-term effects might be. I then (rather foolishly) asked the audience in Edinburgh what they thought of me without glasses and the first heckle was 'psycho killer'. And after thirty-six years of them framing my world view, I've grown rather fond of glasses.

There are side effects. The triad of ginger hair, freckles and glasses leaves you wide open to John Denver/Joe Ninety/Milky Bar Kid abuse. It's harder to snog in specs and your dance movements are a bit restricted. The first time I wore mine to a village hall disco, I lost them two bars into the guitar solo on *Freebird* and it took me an hour to find them. I refused to wear them for a while afterwards, so my sex education behind the French hut was a purple haze.

I was desperate for contact lenses, and at sixteen, I got them. Within a week, I crashed out after a party, put them in a glass of water by the bed, woke with a raging thirst and swallowed them. The optician told me that my insurance didn't cover gross acts of stupidity but I got both of them back with a bit of determination and a sieve. But the old hard contact lenses were hopeless for a junior doctor on call. I couldn't sleep in them and I couldn't spend five minutes putting them in when I was called out to a cardiac arrest. So I switched back to glasses and have stuck with them ever since.

Glasses have lots of health benefits. They stop nasty things going in your eye (rose thorns, squash balls, champagne corks, semen). Cuddly tortoiseshell frames can make you appear more empathic than you really are; little round ones or reading glasses can make you look scholarly. If you're blond or ginger, they add definition to your eyebrows. Also, patients are less likely to punch you if you wear glasses, and if they won't shut up, you can take them off and suck the arm while 'mmmm-ing'. This gives the impression of listening while drifting off into a pleasant blur, before waking up and guessing, 'It's probably a virus.'

Should MPs tell us what they've snorted?

Only if it was bought with public money. I did once ask Boris Johnson (on *Have I Got News For You*) if he'd ever snorted cocaine and he said: 'I tried it once, and I sneezed. It went everywhere. But it was a very, very foolish, naughty, stupid thing to do.' This had a touch of the Clinton 'sucking but not inhaling' defence, but was much funnier. And politically cute, as it took the heat off

David Cameron who was refusing to reveal what went down at the Bullingdon Club.

In Victorian England, politicians were far less coy. Liberal Prime Minister William Gladstone used to take slugs of liquid morphine before rising unsteadily to defend himself in the House of Commons. And even though Queen Victoria complained: 'He always addresses me as if I were a public meeting,' she never took issue with his opiods, probably because she liked to dabble with tincture of cannabis for her period pains. Heroin, cocaine and morphine were all available on prescription and widely dispensed by male doctors to deal with difficult 'lady patients' (and taken by the doctors themselves to cope with the stress of the job).

We admire honesty in politicians but a culture that goes apoplectic over a state-funded trouser press is unlikely to look kindly on a teenage skunk habit. So I suspect politicians won't go public beyond 'the occasional toke at a student party and it did nothing for me.' At least, not until Boris Johnson becomes Prime Minister.

Drugs (and women) were demonised in the UK during the First World War, when alcohol was restricted and troops in London attended cocaine and sex parties (and ended up with an addiction to syphilis). Possession of cocaine and heroin was outlawed in 1916 under the Defence of the Realm Act. If I was going over the top at the Somme, I'd want something to escape reality.

What's the most dangerous recreational drug?

A drug is probably most dangerous when you've got no idea what it is or what dose you're taking. Doctors and nurses kill thousands of people every year by mistake, even though drugs are clearly labelled, because the margins of error are often very small. Take the anaesthetic painkiller Fentanyl. Get the decimal point in slightly the wrong place, or forget to monitor the vital signs closely, and it can be curtains. So to inject supposedly the same drug, sold as 'Apache', in an unknown dose through a dirty needle, in the dark, after three hours of happy hour seems a bit risky.

Nothing causes as much damage as alcohol, but perhaps the most destructive illegal drug is methamphetamine (crystal meth). You can make it yourself from over-the-counter cold remedies (although explosions are common, and a common reason for getting caught). It causes an unbelievably intense and highly addictive euphoria, like a chemical electrode straight into that pleasure centre; an instant escape from hell. It can also make you incredibly horny, yet unable to come. Meth users rarely use condoms, feel less pain and don't know when to stop, so sores, tears, pregnancy and sexually transmitted infections are common. And when the fun's over, you've leeched your brain and lost your self-respect and dignity, leaving a dried-up, depressed, husk with very bad teeth. Until the next fix.

The German military dispensed metamphetamine in the Second World War to take away fear on the front line. When your chance of not making it was 1 in 3, spiked sweeties were enticing, never mind the side effects. You could choose between *Fliegerschokolade* (airmen's chocolate) or *Panzerschokolade* (tank chocolate). Hitler was thought to enjoy a regular fix of crystal to get through the self-doubt and fatigue, but it wasn't much good for his long-term health.

Most of the drug addicts I've met think they were born that way, with brains 'hard-wired' for addiction. But drugs themselves can alter the structure of the brain and lead to addiction. As an addict once said to me: 'You're too late. I've gone from a cucumber to a pickle.' Once you pickle a cucumber, the changes are irreversible and you can never turn it back again. Likewise, long-term drug abuse can change the brain permanently. Once you hit the pickle stage, your cucumber nights are over.

Pickles can still hang round for a while, particularly pickled doctors. We have access to pure drugs in known doses with clean needles. No rubbish cut in, no bleach, no hepatitis or HIV, no hanging round dodgy estates in the dark. But any drug that has an effect also has side effects. No one ever dies of a cannabis overdose but it can make you anxious, dopey, paranoid and more likely to drive into a tree. Pleasure versus harm.

The last person to offer me drugs was a patient. He had 'some good shit' in for Christmas and wanted to share some with me. I checked with the General Medical Council and —incredibly – they have no specific guidelines for patients giving doctors good shit. So I took a small stash, out of politeness, and fed it to the orchids. Amazing flowers this year. Truly mind-blowing.

Is ecstasy really no riskier than horse-riding?

This rather catchy pronouncement came from my friend Professor David Nutt, the chairman of the Advisory Council on the Misuse of Drugs. Apparently 500,000 people a week use ecstasy in the UK, and 30 people a year die after taking it. If you do the maths, your chance of death is 1 in 850,000, which is roughly the same as the combined risk of death from falling off a horse and crashing your car to avoid someone who's fallen off her horse.

But risk is never that simple. In some parts of the UK, horse riding is riskier because people aren't used to horses, and either whizz by too fast or throw missiles at you for amusement. In leafier areas, horse-riders are given a generously wide berth and ecstasy takers are more likely to be stoned. Taking ecstasy is also riskier in the sense that it's illegal, and it's much harder to get arrested for horse-riding (unless you ride bareskin). And ecstasy use may see you hung out to dry in the *Daily Mail*, a punishment seldom seen for trotting an old Exmoor round the block, even if it's just as risky.

Prof. Nutt got a bit of a roasting for his comparison, not for its accuracy but its possible effect. A government advisor saying ecstasy has the same risk as trotting isn't likely to get more people in the saddle, but it might encourage drug taking. 'Get your disco biscuits here. Safe as horses.'

At least with horse riding, you know roughly what you're letting yourself in for. You can reduce the risks by choosing your animal wisely, putting the saddle on properly, adjusting the stirrups, wearing a hard hat and a bright jacket, and steering clear of busy roads. And you can turn back or get off if it starts to bucket down. But once you've swallowed an anonymous tablet of who knows what, you've no idea what you've let yourself in for and no way of escape. And if you take a queer turn, you may not be surrounded by people who have your best interests at heart.

On paper, ecstasy is no more risky than driving 230 miles in a car, riding 6 miles on a motorbike, travelling 6,000 miles by train or mud-wrestling two fat Labradors. But nothing makes you feel more alive, in love and in the moment than a damp snout at both ends.

Where do I find my 'I've had enough' button?

When you're balancing pleasure and pain, there comes a time when the two cross over and you need to bail out. Some lucky people have an automatic 'I've had enough' button (IHEB) buried deep in the forebrain that tells them when to stop drinking and go home before they make a complete arse of themselves or wake up with terminal head throb. They'll often suddenly disappear from parties or the pub, and manage to hail a taxi home without being sick in it.

If you haven't yet evolved an IHEB, or yours is stuck on manual, you need someone to tell you when to stop and to hide your car keys. This won't be any of your button-less mates, who'll all be docking in the snug, but a switched-on friend who's looking out for you. If everyone with an auto IHEB buddied up with everyone without, the UK would be a far pleasanter place to drink in.

2

Doctors' quirks

Doctors are human and creatures of habit, so although medicine is supposed to be based on science, you can still get very variable opinions and experiences from visiting different doctors with the same problem (or even the same doctor on different days). Half-full doctors save lives, half-empty ones merely delay death. I love the quirkiness of doctoring, but far too much of it is done in an anxious rush. Doctors need to slow down, like everyone else, and medicine needs to rediscover its humanity. As a wise old consultant once told me: 'Always take time to smell the patients.'

Do doctors take the same advice and drugs they dish out to patients?

Not always. I know plenty of doctors who are overweight, drink too much alcohol, cycle without a helmet, eat bacon sandwiches, have no idea what their cholesterol level or blood pressure is and refuse to have a flu jab. We do this because we know that if you've got a good job in a country that disposes of its shit properly, you're likely to live to eighty unless you're unlucky. And we're prepared to accept a few risks in return for pleasure and freedom.

The drugs and advice we dish sound mighty impressive when you apply them to the whole population, but the benefits to an individual person seem far more marginal. And some of the things that are bad for you in excess (sun, alcohol, wrestling with Labradors) are good for you in moderation. The trick with risk is to suss out the pros and cons of whatever you fancy, and enjoy it without guilt. But if shit happens, accept it, turn it into a good story and move on.

Some risks and benefits are very hard to predict. An Asian medical student went to a concert in London, a few months after the July bombings, wearing a backpack. He was stopped and searched, and found to be carrying a packed lunch and a couple of spliffs. This could have meant the end of his career but he was an exemplary student and the General Medical Council decided to give him counselling and regular drug testing instead. So now he goes around telling everyone how fabulous the GMC is, which is almost unheard of.

Are doctors full of spin?

Yes, but then so is everyone. There are endless ways that you can frame information to nudge people in one direction or the other. Some patients respond to numbers, some to humour, some to metaphor and some to the sight of the doctor rolling up his sleeve. Medicine is part science, part performance art and part getting you out of the door as quickly as possible at 6pm on a Friday.

Say you've got high cholesterol. Here are a dirty dozen bits of advice you might get, depending on who you see. Some are possibly more 'right' than others, but who's to say what's the best option for a ten-minute consultation in a small, muggy room that reeks of stale coffee and the remains of the previous patient? You decide . . .

1. 'If you take this drug every day for five years your risk of death will be reduced by a whopping 40%. And even if you live, no-one wants to go through a heart attack or a stroke. Open wide!'

2. 'If thirty-three people like you take this drug every day for five years, one death will be prevented and I don't know whether it will be yours. But it seems unlikely. Shall I draw a picture?'

3. 'If 100 people like you are given no treatment for five years, 92 will live and 8 will die. Whether you're one of the 92 or one of the 8 is anybody's guess. Then, if 100 people like you take this drug every day for five years, 95 will live and 5 will die. Again, I've no idea if you're in the lucky 95 or the unlucky 5. Did you get all that? Maybe I'd better open the window.'

4. 'I don't really believe in all this cholesterol bollocks. Just bugger off and enjoy yourself. A dog, a job and a knob. That's all you need.'

5. 'We could all do with lowering our cholesterol but you're already on ten tablets and God knows how they're reacting with each other. Go away and eat lots of vegetables.'

6. 'You must take this drug for the rest of your life or you might die prematurely or suffer chronic ill-health. We'll start you on the cheapest. By the way, you have gorgeous eyes.'

7. 'Did you see the 'goal' on Saturday? It was so far over the line, I though Neil Warnock's head was going to explode. I bet he's got high cholesterol. So have you, by the way, but we've run out of

time to talk about it. Why don't you make an appointment with the nurse? She specialises in body fat.'

8. 'Please take this tablet every day for life. I will earn more money if your cholesterol goes down, and private school fees are increasing 8%, year on year. Could you lend me a fiver?'

9. 'I'm not going to advise you one way or another about your cholesterol. You need to evaluate the risks and benefits for yourself and make your own choice. Here are twenty-seven guidelines. You have precisely three minutes. Do you mind if I open the window?'

10. 'If you swallowed 1,825 tablets at a rate of 1 a day for five years and at a prescription cost of £400, your absolute risk of death would fall by 0.03%. The statistically significant side effects are muscle damage, headache, abdominal pain, nausea, vomiting, hair loss, anaemia, dizziness, depression, nerve damage, hepatitis, jaundice, pancreatitis and hypersensitivity syndrome. Still want some? Shall we try homeopathy instead? Or perhaps you'd prefer to write a poem?'

11. 'Look at these pretty little tablets, aren't they sweet? Little peachy dollops of doctor love, all for you. Please swallow them, just for me. You are my favourite patient, after all. You can sit on my knee and call me daddy if you like.'

12. 'Come outside and look at this. I've made a snake out of all the tablets you'll be gulping down over the next decade and it goes twice around the surgery, up the herbaceous border and back.

And guess where I got all these pills? From the cupboard under the sink of all those patients who died without opening the packets.'

Why do some GPs buzz you and some fetch you?

How doctors summon you is a good indication of how they're going to treat you. Ever since the invention of electricity, buzzing has been the norm for doctors who considered it too secretarial to fetch and carry patients from the waiting room. Early intercoms were not known for their voice quality, and patients were left to guess if they were being called, based on a rough crackle and a few syllables of Dalek.

Modern intercoms go through the telephone network and are of much better sound quality, the only drawback being that if you inadvertently consult with the receiver off the hook, the whole waiting room gets to hear about Mrs Taylor's warty growth.

Many practices use technology to avoid human contact. Some have a big machine that you plug your date of birth into when you arrive, and you're summoned automatically without having to trouble the receptionists (who are far too busy helping the anxious and confused key their dates of birth into the new machine).

Other practices have a not-so-subtle electronic display that flashes up inappropriate digital adverts ('Has your doctor got dirty fingernails? Contact Bennett's solicitors, no win no fee'). And when you're summoned, your name crawls across the screen, like an announcement for the next station, but in lurid LED red. So now everyone knows you've thrown a swine-flu sickie.

To preserve confidentiality, patients can be given an anonymous number, which goes down a treat in the clap clinic

('Morning Vicar.' 'Shhhh — today I'm 157 on the men's side'). Or you can try a more personal touch. One local GP practice gives patients tokens with numbered Beatrix Potter characters on. When there's a buzz, you compare numbers and discover you're behind Appley Dappley but in front of the Flopsy Bunnies. And no-one will ever guess that you, Gemima Puddleduck, are really the vicar.

Personally, I always try fetching in person (FIPing). The early eye contact and cheesy smile can do much to assuage the anxiety of embarrassing itch. FIPing also allows the doctor to secretly observe his next patient through the crack in the waiting room door. Mrs Bishop is doing 'unobserved' handstands in the toy-corner but assumes a look of chronic world-weariness the moment a doctor appears. Why?

FIPing gives you more guessing time with patients, from the moment they try to get out of those ludicrously-low bucket seats to the moment they set foot in your consulting room. Do they look sick? Can they limp without changing legs? How will she fit that double buggy through the door without chipping the paintwork?

I usually see if patients can pass me on the corridor — as much to suss out my level of fitness as theirs — but a colleague is convinced he can dictate the pace and style of his consultations by the manner in which he leads the patients to his room. A leisurely stroll if he's not too pushed for time, a brisk trot if he is. The brisk trot looks like he's concealing a tuberous vegetable, but there might be something in it.

FIPing is particularly useful if someone's left an unfriendly aroma in your room and you need a few moments to clear your head. And patients seem to like it. If they're seeing a familiar doctor, they can pack in an extra minute by addressing the bunions on the landing. And if it's a new doctor, they can decide whether they want to bring up psychological issues (e.g. the husband who locks himself in the closet and sniffs tennis shoes) or stick to the tennis elbow.

In theory, FIPing should also cut down on mistaken identity but for new and amnesiac doctors, it's a source of constant embarrassment. Say your next patient is Mrs Thomas, aged fifty. When you get to the waiting room, there are four women fitting that description. So who do you bestow the all important early eye-contact on? And what if you saw her only last week and haven't the faintest recollection what she looks like? Your only option then is to stare at the linoleum which makes Mrs Thomas think you're not in the least bit interested in her. Also, if none of the women are Mrs Thomas, you can spend a long time staring at the lino. Ten minutes is my record.

Successful FIPing also depends on the geography of the surgery. If it's on six levels you can never get down the stairs because they're blocked with patients who've collapsed on the way up or are just taking a breather. So you end up examining over the banister on Level 3. 'And cough, Vicar.' The other problem with FIPing is that it leaves you no time to do anything in-between patients.

What do doctors do in-between patients?

Split up fights, usually. Sandwiching yourself between patients for pleasure is rare, and the GMC frowns heavily on frottage. When patients finally leave the room, GPs have on average a thirty second turnaround time, but most of that is now spent typing frantically into the computer to claim money for treating whichever disease we're being paid for this week. In the old days, I used to knock off a few pages of something like *Tales of the City* in turnaround time. At 800 words a chapter, there's something very satisfying in polishing off a whole story in-between the worried well. On a bad day, you play catch up. No time to breathe between patients. Years ago, a stressed GP would be writing the previous patient's notes up as you walked in. So no eye contact and a bad start to the consultation. These days, we're hunched over a keyboard and hidden behind a screen. So no eye contact and a bad start to the consultation. That's progress for you.

After a very stressful consultation, we're advised to take a time out, but usually don't, and launch headlong into the next very stressful consultation, conscious of the fact that we're now running forty minutes late. However, this risks transporting the angst from one consultation to the next. Why is the doctor crying behind the computer?

Others try 'stress control techniques'; relaxation, yoga, self-hypnosis, meditation, putting on sandals and growing a beard – you name it, GPs have done it. I know one who keeps a punch bag in the treatment room, but less obtrusive is to squeeze a squidgy stress-reliever that doubles as a prosthetic testicle. Almost as therapeutic as squeezing a real one, and a lot more ethical. Failing that, you'll always find twenty Silk Cut and a packet of Polos in Doctor's secret drawer (third down on the left, behind the rubber nun suit and the tube of body butter. Or is that just me?).

Why do some doctors stare at your face and others at your feet?

It depends on the personality disorder of the doctor. Starers may have mild psychopathic tendencies or just be fresh from my communication skills training. Perhaps they had their eyelids removed in a Freshers' Week prank. Or it may just be a function of the doctor's speciality; anaesthetists spend a lot of time staring at you in the hope you'll wake up, psychiatrists do it to put you to sleep. Or the staring may be down to the fact that you've got something to stare at, like a big lump or jug ears or a Bowie knife.

Doctors who prefer feet to faces aren't always orthopaedic surgeons. A geriatrician once taught me to look at the feet first: 'If a man can do up his shoe-laces, there can't be much wrong with him.' He had a point. Whether you do bunny-ears or snake-around-the-tree, lace tying requires eyesight, balance, flexibility, co-ordination, motivation and memory. But you could still have prostate cancer.

Many foot-starers are the poor sods who sailed into medical school with three Grade A science A levels and the communication skills of a dead skunk. They may glance at you at the beginning of the consultation, but if you've got something awry in the emotional department (grief, anger, despair, hyperventilation), they start shifting in their seats and fidgeting with their fringes and you won't get a whiff of a pupil. They'll happily hide behind a screen and ask you about your cholesterol when you've come in to talk about your dead dog.

Averting eye contact can be entirely appropriate, like when you're banding a haemorrhoid or you stumble across someone undressing. It's an odd thing, undressing. Doctors are allowed to see you buck-naked or fully clothed, but if we catch you in the process of removing your wonder-truss, it becomes horribly inappropriate. The process of de-robing is ritualistically sexy, or at least it might be if we looked.

Outside undressing, observation is the heart of medicine. As one of my consultants used to say: 'The jaw line reveals inheritance, the lips show what life has done to the patient and the eyes reveal the emotions of the moment.' There's far more to looking at someone than spotting a diagnosis. And it's worth observing your doctor too. Why has he got egg in his beard? Does she look sicker than I do? And is he about to trip over his shoelaces? All feedback welcome.

Why do doctors always come at you from the right?

Because we're taught to approach the bed from the left (which is your right), and if you don't do what you're taught to do at medical school, you get kicked out early and bring shame on your family. To be fair, there's more to it than ritual. Most doctors hold the stethoscope in the right hand so leaning over from the left (your right) makes examination of your left-leaning heart (on our right) a bit easier.

Also, wards were usually built with the bedside locker on the patient's right so the religious trinkets would always be on the right. Doctors approaching from that side then had the double whammy of being closer to God and closer to the box of Roses, so we can pocket a few under the pretence of listening to the back of the chest or getting you to look 'up there to your left' or, my favourite:

'Close your eyes and touch your nose with that finger.'

'Why this finger?'

'It just is, alrht?'

'What have you got in your mouth, doctor?'

'Nnnthng.'

Why do doctors do that tapping thing with the fingers?

Percussion isn't tapping, it's a finely-honed skill whereby the left middle finger is placed firmly over the chest wall and struck over the mid-phalanx with the tip of the right middle finger, meeting it smartly at right angles with an easy action of the wrist. You should make a satisfying, resonant, thwacking sound. If you don't, it either means you're not very good at it, or that the lung you're percussing hasn't got enough air in it to resonate. It could be collapsed or full of fluid or infection. Sometimes it can be too resonant, which means air has escaped into the pleural cavity, compressing the lung down and threatening life. Then you stick a needle through the chest wall and let all the air out, just like they do on *Casualty*.

Why do doctors put their hand on your chest and get you to say 'ninety-nine'?

Because the ice-cream man's arrived. And occasionally to assess the transmission of sound vibration through the chest. It's called tactile vocal fremitus, and it tastes better with a flake. Some doctors ask you to whisper ninety-nine, which means you'll never get your ice-cream. But you may not feel like one, because if your lungs are all bunged up, they transmit the quietest voice sounds very well. This is known as whispering pectoriloquy and nobody can spell it.

Do doctors ever pretend to hear noises with a stethoscope?

No, no, no. Yes. Some doctors, especially when we're running late, have decided whether you're getting antibiotics or not for your tickly cough before we lift your shirt up. This isn't necessarily bad medicine – diagnoses are usually made by chatting, and the examination is often just for show. If a doctor wants to justify giving you antibiotics when she knows she probably shouldn't but you've made it pretty clear you're not leaving without them, she'll probably invent 'a few crackles at the base'. On the other hand, if he only ever gives out penicillin for syphilis, he may well choose to ignore the wheezing, rubbing and crackling that's keeping the neighbours awake.

The stethoscope has huge cultural significance in medicine. Some doctors wear one down the pub, just so you know. One year it's cool to let it dangle around your neck, the next you drape it round your shoulders or, if you're really cocky, you swirl it in large circles to attract the nurses (this never worked for me). Stethoscopes now come in all colours and some are so expensive they claim to let you hear the whole body at once.

If you're really lazy or pushed for time, you don't need to get patients to undress at all. You just make a small rhombus between the second and third buttons and, with a very long stethoscope, there's no body cavity you can't pretend to reach. For most us, they're just guessing tubes that buy us a bit of time while we think about how to wind up the consultation.

NOTE: The most useful use of a stethoscope is to reverse it and use it as a hearing aid. Put it in the patient's ears and speak through the bell. It works a treat but is perhaps a bit too obtrusive for long-term use.

What did GPs do in the days before they dished out pills?

Reassurance mainly. In my black bag, next to the half-eaten sandwiches and the half-empty bottle of vodka, is a fabulous book called *Good General Practice*, published in 1954, and chock full of paternalistic tips that I'm not quite brave enough to follow:

1. All practices have their share of neurotics. Some are born, but many are made by the medical profession. If you are not sure what is wrong, do not hint at the worst and give a really gloomy prognosis just to safeguard yourself. Patients try to live up to their prognosis.

2. Patients set great store on their hearts. A hint from their doctor that all is not well with the heart will start a chain of worry which cannot be

dispelled by any number of later reassurances. Remember that over the age of 70, most hearts are enlarged and many have a murmur and a mild degree of cardiac failure. Tell a man that his heart is 'excellent for his age' or 'good for another twenty years' and he will have a new lease of life.

3. If you can possibly avoid it, do not tell patients that they have high blood pressure. It is tantamount to telling them they are on the point of having a stroke. High blood pressure causes no symptoms until the patient knows he has it. Thereafter there is no end to the symptoms. Once you know it is high, there is little point in taking repeated readings. It only concentrates the patient's attention to it. Many people with normal blood pressure have strokes, and many people with high blood pressure live to extreme old age.

Now that we have effective treatments for heart failure and high blood pressure, and even more effective lawyers to sue us if we get it wrong, we tell patients everything and accentuate the negative to cover our arses. And because we do it from behind a computer with no eye contact in under ten minutes, patients leave the room with profound anxiety and a prescription for half a dozen drugs many have no intention of taking. The few that do often feel queer on so many pills. There's no point in living longer if you don't feel better.

What's the most irritating thing a doctor can say to a patient?

I know a doctor who says to male patients: 'What's the problem?' and to female patients: 'What seems to be the problem?' That would be hard to beat in the irritating stakes, although 'Your body is a temple, it's not a toy' runs it close.

When a doctor rolls up his sleeve is it time to leave?

It's certainly time to ask what happens next. Particularly if he also flicks his tie over his shoulder. These days, all hospital doctors are supposed to be both tie-less and bare below the elbows all the time, allegedly to reduce the risk of infection, but it makes them look as if they're on constant rubber glove standby.

Is it OK to swear in front of patients?

I'm a big fan of slang but then I am half-Australian, where even the c-word can be a term of endearment. Not everyone agrees. Breezing through an old *Nursing Times* on the bog (sorry, toilet), I came across a nurse who 'escaped with a caution' for using 'vulgar and explicit language' in front of patients. The nurse defended the use of the word 'cock' to describe a penis at a Kent nursing home: 'I've used it many times before and do not believe it to be disgusting. I was a tomboy as a child and have always sworn a bit.' The nurse also admitted to referring to two patients as 'bastards' and owned up to a 'bum'. However she denied telling a sixty-year-old woman eating a banana, 'It must be a long time since you sucked on one of those.'

I was loitering in reception once and I heard a GP say, over the intercom, 'Come in Mrs Jones, you big jelly belly. Get your big flabby arse in here.' Everybody laughed, including Mrs Jones (at least in public). Maybe doctors get away with more than nurses, or maybe just this doctor because he'd been at the practice for thirty years and sussed out who he could be rude to. As a locum, you can't waltz into an unfamiliar waiting room firing 'jelly belly' from the hip. But there may still be room for slang in the consultation. Many patients are confused not just by the meaning of life but the meaning of bowels. How much less confusing it would be if we could say 'poo', 'turd' or 'big job' without fear of ending up in front of the GMC. That's how I'll be defending this book when the bastards come and get me.

What do doctors do with patients they hate?

Put them into football teams. I once worked in a practice where all the toughest patients were put into a team of the week, displayed in the coffee room. If you got a really difficult bugger, you were secretly pleased because you could run in and put him straight in at left back. But before you could make a substitution, you had to justify it to the other doctors, which was a clever way of getting you to articulate what was so tough about the consultation.

GPs used to talk about 'heartsink' patients (people who make your heart plummet the moment you spot them on your morning list) and a psychiatrist called Groves even split them up into four groups (manipulative help-rejecters, self-destructive deniers, entitled demanders and dependent clingers). But there are plenty of heartsink doctors too, and when a consultation goes tits up, there are issues on both sides.

Just as parents aren't supposed to say they hate their children, only that they find their behaviour challenging, so it is with doctors. Here's a rundown from a GP meeting I went to recently of what different GPs find difficult. It says as much about the doctor as the patient.

1. 'As a female GP, I see mainly women and children, and men are a rarity. The ones I find difficult are the business-like older men. They make me feel inadequate, and I'm not sure why. Perhaps I don't see enough of them to feel confident, but I find it very hard to tune into their wavelength. I'm sure they perceive me either as a nurse, or of lower status than a male GP, and it's not uncommon for them to try to pull rank over me.'

2. 'I'm the token man in my practice and I get really thrown if a woman comes to see me to discuss HRT. I think 'Why me? What's going on here?' I know it may just be that I've seen them for something else and they're being loyal, or perhaps they prefer seeing a male doctor. But I'm not convinced. I mean, what woman in her right mind would go to a man to discuss vaginal dryness?'

3. 'I find it hard to deal with other educated, middle-class professionals. They tend to be more demanding, less grateful, less tolerant of the shortcomings of the NHS. And they're used to being in control - I find it very difficult to get the doctor-patient relationship right.'

4. 'I get stressed out by people who come in with a great list of diffuse symptoms covering practically every body system. And then the bloody computer flashes up a whole list of targets I have to hit. A wave of despair comes over me – how the hell can I sort this lot out in 10 minutes?'

5. 'If anyone comes in and demands that

'something must be done' it immediately gets my back up. Usually it's a relative rather than a patient, and often they feel guilty because they themselves haven't done more. It really grates when they live 200 miles away, do a flying visit on mother once a year and then throw a wobbly about the state she's in. It makes me angry because they're implying I'm not doing my best – but I also worry in case I'm not.'

6. 'I hate patients who think – or pretend – they are your friends when you don't know them from Adam. They call you by your first name to try to worm their way into your affections. Perhaps they think they'll get better treatment, but it just puts me off.'

7. 'Doctors as patients are really stressful, especially when they're consultants. I immediately get stuck in the roll of junior colleague and I feel like I'm being tested all the time. It's even worse if they consult about their own specialty – I've just seen a chest physician with a cough.'

'What did you say?'

'There's a lot of it about.'

'And?'

'It's probably a virus – but then I ordered loads of inappropriate tests and X-rays. You know – because he was a consultant . . .'

8. 'I'm very uneasy seeing members of staff as patients. I mean, they know what we're really like. They hear all the bitching in the coffee room. The doctors are all registered at other

practices, but no-one else. I once had to do a rectal examination on the practice manager . . .'

9. 'I hate picking up another doctor's mess. Last week, I saw a woman who'd been in hospital for a routine operation. I hadn't had a letter back from the surgeon so I asked, 'What did the doctor tell you?' 'He said I was going home to die.' She looked quite well on it, but I presumed they'd found something awful when they'd opened her up so we had a long chat about making wills and pain relief. When I got back to the surgery, I called the doctor for more details. He was very surprised and very Australian. 'I told her she was going home today.'

Do unlucky beds really exist?

Possibly. Many patients reckon they've spotted a bed, usually opposite, where all the occupants are wheeled out in a shroud but in any given period, one bed will be the unluckiest by chance alone. Whether there's more to it than that depends on local circumstance. A bed with an infected mattress is bad news. If it's furthest from the nurses' station, it can be hard to get attention when you really need it. If it's furthest from the sink or spray, the staff may not wash their hands.

Sometimes the cleaner will pull out one particular plug to do the vacuuming. Or perhaps just one nurse always looks after patients in that bed, and she's a little bit careless. Or worse. Or the bed could be nearest to the exit and nurses deliberately put people there who are about to die so it's easier for the porters to sneak them out. Or you might have tunnel vision so you only notice what's going on in the bed opposite. Or maybe the whole ward's conspiring to play a cruel practical joke on you and the patients opposite are just pretending to be dead. Whatever the reason, it's worth doing a bit of research before you label a bed unlucky.

Do doctors still remove bits of brain with an ice-pick?

I suspect someone is trying it right now as a cheap alternative to waterboarding, but the last supposedly therapeutic lobotomy with ice-pick in an apparently civilised country was performed in America in 1967, by neurologist Dr Walter Freeman. Freeman clocked up nearly 3,500 lobotomies in his lifetime, without having any surgical qualifications. And he wasn't an anaesthetist either. He knocked patients out with electricity, pulled back an eyelid, pushed in and up with the ice-pick, whacked it with a rubber mallet through the orbital bone and into the brain, sliced through the frontal lobe and yanked it out again. His 'patients' were apparently conscious again – if a little unsteady and confused – in under 10 minutes. A mobile, production line lobotomy service using a household tool with *Uline Ice Company* emblazoned on the side.

To be fair, the treatment of the severely mental ill in Freeman's time was pretty barbaric all-round. Psychiatric hospitals were known as snake pits and jammed full of patients locked away for a lifetime. Some were tied up and force fed, with mouths clamped open. There was shit smeared all over the walls, terrible overcrowding and a never ending rise in demand. And this was America, not the NHS.

In the 1940s, treatment largely revolved around shocking patients, either with ECT without anaesthesia or forced chemical convulsions. Freeman decided to go one step further and rewire the brain permanently. It was just a theory, but a Portuguese

45

surgeon called Egas Moniz was getting 'interesting' results by leucotomy (removing chunks of brain with a device like an apple corer) and got a very dubious Nobel Prize for his efforts.

Freeman developed his eye socket approach and used it on, amongst many others, the sister of John F Kennedy. He criss-crossed America and Europe in a camper van, plying his trade, often moving on before his patients relapsed or died. In the mid-fifties he moved to California, offering lobotomies to neurotic housewives and disruptive children. By then, there was ample evidence that his treatment was harmful and he was largely discredited by the establishment. But he believed in what he was doing, patients trusted him and nobody stopped him until he was 72 years old. Doctors, like politicians and bankers, were never good at regulating themselves.

Do doctors still experiment on themselves?

Doctors (and medical students) will occasionally volunteer to try out new drugs in controlled trials, but in the days before trials, heroic doctors would often have a go first before trying things out on their patients. In 1943 Swiss chemist Dr Albert Hoffman swallowed the drug extract of a fungus which he hoped would help people with breathing difficulties. Unfortunately, the drug preferred to camp out in his mind, giving him vivid hallucinations on his bike ride home. 'It was so unusual that I really got afraid that I had become insane . . .' Albert had discovered LSD and taken the world's first trip. Not quite enough for a Nobel Prize, but ever-lasting adoration from the world's acid heads.

No Nobel Prize either for Dr Pierre Bestain, who was so convinced he'd discovered the antidote to Death Cap mushroom that he wolfed a whole plateful, fried with a knob of butter. He survived and word soon spread of his amazing antidote. Alas, when others tried it to treat unintentional overdoses, it failed without fail. Pierre, it seems, was just genetically immune to the mushrooms.

One person's experience doesn't quite constitute scientific proof; you need to road test your wonder drug on more than your own gene pool before you flog it to the public. Being your own guinea pig has its limits and it's not without considerable risk, but if you pull it off, you'll go down in history.

Step forward my medical hero and fellow Australian, Dr Barry Marshall. Barry was convinced that the bacteria Helicobacter pylori caused stomach ulcers, but back in 1982 his peers thought he was away with the fairies. So he asked his mate John Noakes (no relation to Shep) to knock him up a heavy suspension of the bug scraped straight off the agar plate. And he sculled it, down in one. 'It's not the sort of thing you'd want to sip. It was like swamp water, quite putrid in fact . . .' Way to go, mate.

And he did. He woke at 3am with terrible stomach cramps and started a lengthy affair with his toilet. On day eight, he woke at 6am and had a curious vomit: 'I couldn't taste any acid. It looked just like water I was bringing up, but I hadn't been drinking anything so it was quite puzzling.' The bacteria had caused all the protective acid to disappear out of his gastric juice. After ten days of suffering, a celebratory endoscopy found early signs of a stomach ulcer.

'Unfortunately, my wife insisted I start taking antibiotics after that because she was worried about me getting worse or something bad happening . . .' Antibiotics cured the ulcer, Barry got a Nobel Prize and further research proved that eradicating the bug not only cures stomach ulcers but stops relapses.

If you're not quite brave enough to experiment on yourself, there's always your children. Gerhard Domagk, a pioneer of sulphonamide antibiotics, tried them out on his daughter first, and Edward Jenner treated his son to an inoculation of cow pox liquid to test his vaccination theories. Both got away with it and to this day, doctors can be found giving their kids antibiotics when they tell everyone else to try Calpol.

Has a doctor ever eaten a patient's poo?

We do it all the time, as a punishment for not washing our hands properly, but the only wanton poo-eater on record is Dr Joseph Goldenberg of the US Public Health Service. Dr G wanted to find out the cause of pellagra, a disease that sounds like a pasta dish but kills you with diarrhoea, dermatitis and dementia. In America, where pellagra had previously been rare, suddenly there were huge and totally unexplained outbreaks. Hundreds of people died. As the *Journal of the American Medical Association* concluded in 1914, it was 'in all probability a specific infectious disease communicable from person-to-person by means at present unknown'.

Like a good scientist, Goldenberg decided to prove pellagra was infectious by experiment. He started off gently, extracting blood from one of his pellagra patients and injecting it into his own shoulder. Then he collected phlegm and snot from the mouth and nose of the patient and rubbed it into his own mouth and nose. Nausea, vomiting, bloody diarrhoea, depression, psychosis and scaly skin awaited Goldenberg if his experiment worked. It didn't.

Goldenberg naturally concluded he hadn't gone far enough. Three days later he decided to swallow some sodium bicarbonate to neutralise the acid in his stomach and maximise his chance of getting infected. Then he swallowed, in turn, samples of urine, faeces and skin taken from his obliging if slightly puzzled patient. Unsurprisingly he got one of the 3 Ds, diarrhoea, but he didn't develop pellagra.

A few days later he managed to persuade four close friends to join him in eating skin, faeces and urine from a pellagra patient. Must have been one hell of a dinner party. His wife was keen to join in but Goldenberg couldn't face the thought of her eating another man's skin and shit. So he injected her with blood taken from a woman dying of pellagra. But none of his posse got the disease.

Goldenberg repeated this experiment an impressive seven times, before convincing himself that this was not an infectious disease. After many years of research, he tracked down a cure: brewers' yeast. Pellagra was caused by a shortage in the diet of the B vitamin niacin and the reason for the outbreak also became clear. At the turn of the century people had changed their eating habits, going from wholemeal grain to fancier and finer ground grain. Unfortunately this process also removed some essential vitamins, crucially niacin. With niacin added back in, the pellagra epidemic disappeared. Good for Goldenberg.

Why do men become gynaecologists?

In the days when all doctors were men, all gynaecologists obviously were too. A few may have chosen the specialty for dubious motives but, having done a few gynaecology outpatient sessions myself, there's nothing remotely titillating about it. Most of the male gynaecologists I've met just have a fascination for the subject.

This enthusiasm was first documented by J. Marion Sims, a bloke despite the name, who practised surgery in Alabama in the nineteenth century and is credited as the founder of modern gynaecology. Of one patient with a fistula (an abnormal connection between vagina and bladder) he wrote: 'Introducing the bent handle of a spoon I saw everything as no man had ever seen before. The fistula was as plain as the nose on a man's face.'

You might query his note-taking but it's fair to say that Sims enjoyed his work. He may have liked looking, but with detached objectivity not lust. He invented a speculum, a catheter, several new surgical techniques and even kept a straight face when a patient 'was embarrassed by an explosive sound of air'. A true professional.

There are now far more women in medicine and gynaecology, and you've got a good chance of being treated by a female doctor, even more so if you ask. But the sex of a doctor is far less important than the manner.

3

Rude health

A lot of people have hang-ups about what hangs down, which is a great pity because it's usually based on misinformation and it stops you enjoying your dangly bits.

HIS BITS

Penis or Tummy Banana?

Penis, definitely, or one of the non-threatening alternatives. Telling your son that he's growing a tummy banana sows the seeds for later inadequacy (unless you banish bananas from the house, which would be a shame because they're an excellent source of potassium). If you can't manage a penis, there's a plethora of relatively harmless substitutes in the willy mould. Chipolata is easy enough to live up to (if it grows, it grows). Avoid anything that suggests aggression, even if you are a butcher (pork-sword, lamb-dagger, mutton-cudgel, beef-bayonet). Some women have an unfortunate habit of giving the penis a proper name as if it had a mind of its own. This is just about tolerable, apart from Justin, which is clearly an insult. Generally men and boys are happy and relaxed about naming and fondling their genitals. Indeed, they're so important that the cricket box was introduced a full century ahead of the safety helmet (1874 vs. 1974). It pays to look after your penis, but it's not much use without a brain. Or maybe it's the other way round.

Should I prick my pearly penile papules?

No. If you pull a young man's foreskin back (**TIP:** ask first), you may find a row of small white pimples, like pretty maids, around the base of the glans (i.e. the bottom edge of Darth Vader's helmet). They're perfectly normal glands that help lubrication and they don't benefit from any interference.

What do 90% of British men have that 70% of American men don't?

A foreskin. Or an appreciation of irony. Score one mark for each. A foreskin contains most of fine touch receptors of the penis. Ironic, then, that anyone would want to chop it off. If you're lucky enough to still have one, hold onto it.

What's a Helix mark?

It's a little red line about an inch across, just above the base of the penis. Most adolescent men go through a phase of ramming a six-inch ruler into their pubic arena in the hope of convincing themselves that their erection nudges six inches. The term was coined by the sports' journalist, Old Etonian and Guinness-trial lawyer, Will Buckley who assures me that the practice was widespread at his old school. It is also endemic in state schools, although it tends to be more of a communal affair as there is rarely more than one ruler per classroom.

Why does my scrotum look fifty years older than I do?

Because you're still a young man, you lucky bastard. The scrotum has wrinkles for air-conditioning, which keeps the testicles a degree or so cooler than the rest of the body and makes your sperm less likely to fall asleep on the job. The scrotum also provides a handy test for stress, sleep deprivation and premature ageing. It's a simple comparison to make. Get the little fellas out, look in the mirror and spot the difference. If you can't, slow down and catch up on your sleep.

NOTE: Dr Phil's Scrotal Discrimination Test is not endorsed by anyone official, but it's a lot cheaper than BUPA health screening and it doesn't cost much to set up a testicular drop-in centre. Or you can just share them with friends. Pass them round the cabinet, Gordon. Maybe a hasty reshuffle. Now get some kip.

Why is my scrotum covered in chicken skin?

Evolutionary confusion. Your bollocks hang down like the front end of a turkey, so why not take on its skin? You could also cover them in bread sauce for a Christmas treat. Just go easy on the stuffing.

Does my penis have higher blood pressure than I do?

When it's erect, yes, which is why we measure blood pressure around your arm and not your penis (otherwise you'd all be on medication and we'd all be up before the GMC). A normal resting human blood pressure peaks at 140 mm of mercury, but a really firm erection can manage ten times this. A bull's penis apparently bulges at 1,700, a stallion does 4,000 and the mighty goat comes in at a staggering 7,000 millimetres of mercury. For more information on how this is measured, see *Reproduction in Domesticated Animals* by Gordon James King.

Does a penis always look smaller from above?

Yes. Unless you've got it on the wrong way round.

Are erections powered by laughing gas?

Not quite. Laughing gas in nitrous oxide, N_2O, has two nitrogens attached to one oxygen. The most important molecule in kick-starting an erection is nitric oxide, NO, which has just one atom of each in its molecule. It's a subtle but important difference – if laughing gas was released immediately an erection appeared, then the erection would likely wilt and the human race would die out. Instead, N_2O is used to power rocket engines, but also works as a pain-killer, anaesthetic and – in combination with oxygen – it helps you laugh through and forget childbirth (and it's not just for dads).

NO is such an important chemical messenger in mammals that it was named 'molecule of the year' in 1992. It's responsible for smooth muscle relaxation that allows blood to rush into the penis. It does this by activating a guanylate cyclase second messenger system. This converts guanosine triphosphate into cyclic guanosine monophosphate (cGMP), which in turn activates the sodium pump and opens potassium channels, causing a decrease in intracellular calcium which facilitates smooth muscle relaxation. Erectile dysfunction drugs selectively inhibit PDE5, a cGMP-specific isoenzyme that normally breaks down cGMP. In doing so, they increase the amount of cGMP triggered by the NO pathway. It would be so much simpler if we had a bone in our penis.

Why don't men have a bone in the penis?

A lot of mammals do have a penis bone that make them good to go at any time but primates have evolved theirs out, relying instead on a few spongy tubes and a ridiculously complicated system of hydraulic pumping that requires the full cooperation of both the cardiovascular and nervous systems to get a decent head of pressure. Unsurprisingly, it's prone to all sorts of mechanical failure.

This is either God's little joke, or a clever process of natural selection that allows women to spot the healthiest men. Men who have no trouble getting an erection are generally psychologically and physically healthy and would make a good father (if only they could learn to keep it in their loin cloth). Conversely, those with erectile dysfunction (ED) often have psychological issues, physical illness, financial worries, a ten-gallon cider habit or are just getting on in years.

Fortunately, we now have a remedy for evolution in the shape of assorted pumps, injections, implants and pills, but ED remains a good marker for other illnesses so it's worthwhile going to a doctor and getting an MOT rather than buying cheap blue tablets over the internet that are half horsehair, half pigmy-elephant droppings.

NOTE: The main argument against a penis bone is that some men and women might want sex all the time, and that could get slightly tedious. Maybe evolution isn't so stupid.

Can a normal knob be bent and twisted?

Yes. It's all a matter of degree. If you get your protractor out, you'll find most erections have a slight curve (not that many men will let you measure it). Penises often also have a slight twist (usually anti-cockwise). One in a hundred men bend more than 25 degrees and have Peyronie's disease, named after the physician to King Louis XV. But banana man is as old as the hills, proudly depicted in sculptures dating back to the 6th century BC.

Whether you do anything about it depends on whether it hurts or spoils your enjoyment. Sometimes it straightens itself in time, but if yours won't, take a digital photo of your erection and share it with your GP (far easier than showing what you mean in the flesh). Most penises can be straightened out by surgery.

Do most men have moobs?

Man boobs are pretty much the norm as we've got progressively plumper. Not only do the breasts get fatty, but the fat makes oestrogen which causes the breast tissue to grow. Alcohol lowers testosterone and raises oestrogen, so overweight drinkers can have quite large breasts, but they shrink back if you cut down.

Healthy teenage boys often get temporary moobs, because of fluctuating testosterone levels which aren't always high enough to balance the oestrogen. The breasts tend to shrink again from fifteen onwards. It's also common to feel a firm, tender, rubbery disc at the back of the nipple on both breasts. A lump or enlargement on one side needs checking out – it's rare, but even men can get breast cancer. Some drugs cause moobs, and if yours are huge, your GP may check your hormone levels or refer you to a specialist.

Older men get moobs as our testosterone levels fall and more of the body becomes fat. These are hard to shift, but actually quite attractive if covered with a thick coating of ginger hair.

Why do men pee all over the floor?

A few men pee on the floor deliberately, knowing some poor sod will mop up after them, but we inadvertently miss the target through any combination of haste, desperation, excitement, distraction, poor aim, prostate problems, cold weather, a wart bang in the end of a hole, a side hole, failing memory, a killer loo seat or a foreskin with a mind of its own. We then pretend not to notice what we've done or, just as worrying, genuinely don't notice that the next occupant will have many rivers to cross.

Some problems are easier to fix than others. A loo seat that might fall and decapitate you at any moment is a clear disincentive to raising it, so you end up with pee on the seat, as well as splatter on the floor (and further run-off if the seat is raised afterwards to hide the fact it's been peed on and you're too lazy to wipe it off). A dodgy seat can generally be sorted with refastening an inch or so forwards so it has more lean-back. And a wart can be frozen off.

Peeing with an erection is always a challenge. Nature closes the wee gate to open the sperm gate, so it can take a while to come through but there may still be enough upward elevation to send the stream a good foot high. Sitting down and pressing down can help. Emptying the bladder before (and after) sex is a good idea for both men and women.

Men's aim and concentration is easily improved by giving them something to aim at. At Amsterdam's Schiphol airport, there are flies beautifully engraved into the target area of each trap in the gents' urinal. Without realizing it, you're prompted to hit the spot, a tactic which has reduced spillage and splash-back by some eighty per cent.

Foreskins and end-holes can occasionally get gummed up with normal secretions, causing a split stream that then usually settles into one. The stumpier man may get a pubic hair caught in the end, which can divert the stream sideways but is easily picked off. Permanent split streams happen when the opening or urethra is scarred or damaged, and needs a medical opinion. Ballooning of a tight foreskin can play havoc with a boy's aim but circumcision is rarely necessary and most foreskins go back in time. It may just be a case of sitting down to pee until it does.

Most men have an opening at the end of the penis but some are born with it on the underside and if their parents miss it, they're often too embarrassed to seek help. It can be fixed, but you need to find a specialist. *(see **Does anyone else have a hole on the underside?**)* Prostate problems are probably the commonest cause of poor aim and even incontinence in men, but there's plenty that can be done for that too *(see **Can I examine my own prostate?**)*.

Men tend to focus on one thing at a time, so a quick pee taken during the ad break is likely to end up half in the pan, half out; no flush, no hand-wash and no realisation of the carnage left behind. A strict policy of mopping up your own pee is worth a shout, as is a big sign with 'please don't piss all over the floor' (although a man's aim may go awry as he lifts his head to read it).

Are some men genitally unaware?

Self-pleasure aside, some men seem blissfully unaware of what's going on down below. How could anyone expect you to put something in your mouth that looks and smells like a pensioner's leg smeared in last year's Stilton and stored in a hot tent? But we all know someone who does.

A friend of mine leaves two bars of soap by the sink in the master en suite, one labelled 'for hands', the other 'for foreskin'. It's a nice touch that may one day clinch the sale of the house, but from a hygiene point of view it's a step too far. Rigorous soaping in both men and women can lead to a chemical irritation that mimics an infection *(see **Are some men genitally too aware?**)*. Foreskins just need gentle peeling back in water, a removal of the white stuff and then a dabbing dry, or airing of the glans, before replacement (fungus tends to thrive where it's damp and moist).

Testicular cancer is the commonest cancer in men between the ages of twenty and thirty-five, but it's often women who spot it first, when they're down that way and trying to hurry things up a bit. Less than four per cent of scrotal lumps turn out to be cancer, but they all need checking out, sooner rather than later. The normal scrotum has a bag of worms in it (a combination of sperm collecting tubes and sometimes varicose veins), but cancer occurs in the testicle itself, often starting out as a grain of sand before developing into a definitive lump. Or you may just get a sharp pain, a dull ache or a general heaviness in the scrotum. Either way, show it to a doctor – preferably in the surgery, not the supermarket (although some supermarkets have doctors in them now. And check-outs for six symptoms or less).

Any abnormal discharge also needs checking (the white stuff that shoots out at some speed accompanied by a feeling of intense well-being is perfectly normal, at least in private). Men with sexually transmitted infections often have the dangerous triad of pretending not to notice, hating going to the doctor and hoping it will go away. A man with gonorrhoea can be dripping with pus, getting it all over his shorts and the chaise longue, and still expect to have sex. Don't join in until you're both checked out, treated and given the all clear.

Are some men genitally too aware?

Yes. Like many of life's variables, genital awareness is distributed on a bell-shaped curve, with those happily caked in last year's smegma at one end, and those with chemical burns from obsessive over-washing at the other. You should never separate the penis from the person (no matter how angry you are), and anxiety often accompanies a pristine pole. Some men become obsessive squeezers, gripping the shaft repeatedly to convince themselves that they have a discharge. Unsurprisingly, the penis gets sore and inflamed. Washing with soap on the outside is fine, but shower gel or bleach squirted down the hole can really sting. And pipe cleaners are best left for cleaning pipes.

HER PIECES

Vagina or furry hoop?

I'm a vagina and vulva man, myself. Parents rarely agree on what to name their children, never mind their children's genitals. Daughters present a particular challenge if you're shy about anatomy. One person's 'mee mee' is another's 'moo moo', 'fu fu', 'felooloo', 'tuppence', 'bits and bobs', 'down below', 'Mary', 'front bottom', 'little twinkle', 'blossom', 'vajayjay', 'jina' or 'leg pit'. And let's not forget the (cockney rhyming) 'fine china'. 'Minge', 'fanny' and 'twat' just don't sound right, and neither does the 'C' word, even when it's said in an Australian accent.

None of these dispel the common anatomical confusion about what's in and what's out. *The Vagina Monologues*, an iconic play aimed at allowing women to reclaim their genitals, spends much of the time musing on the vulva. The vagina is tucked away inside and the labia (fleshy lips, two pairs) and clitoris (pearly button of joy) are all vulva. There's even a mons venerens, a vestibule and a fourchette in a vulva, if only we knew where to look.

Nobody uses 'vulva' in polite discourse, nobody's quite sure what it means and nobody likes to mention that women are beautifully designed for surface joy without a visit from Mr Dyno-Rod. If you can't manage vagina and vulva over Cornflakes, try V and V. It at least sows the seed that there's more to be found than an opening, and it's perfectly OK to go exploring (but finish your Cornflakes first).

If women had to climax to produce an egg, would humans die out?

Certainly there'd be fewer of us, but that may not be a bad thing. And men who wanted to be fathers would have to try harder (as if producing an erection every time a thermometer says so isn't hard enough).

Does a clitoris have legs?

Yes. There's far more to a clitoris than meets the eye. As Frank Skinner observed: 'It's about the only thing with a hood I'm not frightened of these days.' It's also got lips, ligaments, a glans, a shaft, a sponge, a bulb, a diaphragm, a good blood supply and around 8,000 nerve endings, so if you do manage to find it, don't overdo the celebrations. It's likely to be extremely sensitive. Ask before you touch. And don't drop it.

Why can't women pee standing up?

Women can pee standing up perfectly well, as anyone who's viewed the world from under a coffee table will testify. But due to certain anatomical constraints, they can't go it alone without baring themselves. There are however a number of ingenious urination aids on the market, such as Shewee, a moulded plastic funnel which you place discretely under the crotch, with underwear pushed aside, to divert the flow in a man-wards manner. This allows you to pee upright or squatting without getting a chilly arse and you don't have to touch base with disgusting public or portable toilets. You could, for a laugh, go into the gents and pee all over the floor like a man. I haven't tried Shewee but I'm told it's rather good (although the website does oversell it: 'Travel the world with the comfort of home in your pocket.' Yeah, right). Other brands are available (Wizz-away, P-mate etc. etc.).

Does jogging make your boobs droop?

Can do. One study found that when women jog, your breasts move 'in a three dimensional figure of eight', as if you needed another reason for men to stare at them. Depending on the weight and shape of your breasts, you can even calculate the size of the strain on the supporting tissues, but suffice to say that the average 36C, 300 gram breast will sag a bit with prolonged jogging. On a brighter note, bounce and sag can be reduced greatly with a very supportive sports bra.

Does breast size matter to men?

Much less than you think. Most men find all breasts and nipples attractive, whatever their size or shape, and whether or not they've got a few hairs on. And we'd hate to inhabit a world where all breasts looked identical.

Is it worth having a nip, tuck and tidy down below?

The vulval lips come in a wonderful variety of shapes and sizes. Sometimes the outer ones are bigger than the inner ones, sometimes it's the other way round. One way to find the clitoris it to trace the outer lips until they meet at the top, and peer gently under the hood. Another is to ask. Just as men are given performance anxiety by porn-fed cucumbers, some women feel their vulvas have to be non-protruding. But who's going to notice? Most men have enough trouble remembering your birthday, so they're hardly likely to recall the shape of your vulva (the average time spent down that way is thirteen seconds, eyes shut and accompanied by a prayer).

If you want advice, start by going to the local sexual health clinic. They've seen every shape of vulva going and they're pretty good at reassurance. Remember, nothing hangs like a scrotum and you don't see men lining up to have theirs clipped. If you're sure you want some form of reshaping, ask the clinic to recommend a cosmetic surgeon who knows what he or she is doing. The genitals are no place for a dabbler.

If women had no discharge, would they squeak?

No. There are no hinges in a vagina, but lots of lubrication. The vagina stays moist to clean itself, and the healthy discharge clears out dead cells and bacteria. Don't help it along with soap or douching – this just causes soreness and thrush. The discharge comes from glands at the neck of the womb and is clear or white, and painless. We all have our own natural odour, and curry and asparagus can apparently affect women down there. The discharge is acidic to fight infection and some women believe that pineapple (orally) adds to the acidity and makes them taste more fruity. No large trial has confirmed or refuted this.

Discharge normally varies in amount and consistency during the cycle: non-existent or thick at the start; clear, slippery and sperm-friendly in the middle as the egg is released. It oxidises in air, so it's not uncommon to find a yellow-brown stain on your pants mid-cycle that's easy to confuse with blood. If your discharge is itchy, very smelly or a new colour (white, yellow or green), it can nearly always be cured by a trip to the right doctor. And it's always worth feeling around for a forgotten tampon.

BITS AND PIECES

Can you beat a good poo?

Not easily. The anus is a wonderful piece of kit and well worth keeping in shape. Thanks to its intricate sphincter and rich nerve supply, it tells you when you need a poo and generally makes it very enjoyable to hold on for a bit. Then when the 'call to stool' becomes overwhelming, all you need to do is sit forward and relax. Your amazing anus can also tell the difference between a solid, a liquid and a gas, and usually gets it right first time (unless you've got gastroenteritis, when a sly fart can quickly develop into something more substantial).

Unfortunately, your anus can't tell you how badly your poo is going to stink until it's too late, but then often neither can you. As the Icelandic proverb goes: 'Every man likes the smell of his own farts', so even if you've been firing off warning shots to others all morning, you may have experienced nothing more than a soothing inhalation.

Poo smells because the bacteria in it produce sulphurous gases. Why man-poo stinks more than lady-poo is something of a mystery. In evolutionary terms, it could simply be marking out your territory. Perhaps the smell evolved as a warning to hunter-gatherers to not confuse a turd with a truffle. Or it may just be that men consume more of the things that make poo really stink (meat, fat, beer, beans).

Some men are strangely proud of a spectacularly bad odour, but if it's getting to be a relationship breaker, there are a number of options:

- Close the door and open the window. Strange as it seems, less than half of men do both.

- Flush and go. Flush the toilet the second the shit hits the pan. Only partially successful, you end up with a wet bum and it takes a lot of the pleasure away.

- Burn off the gas. Posh houses often have a box of matches on top of the loo-roll holder. You don't have to ignite the gas as soon as it comes out (spectacular, but a high risk of singeing), merely burn it off when you've finished. Again, the sooner you do it the better, and the closer you get it to the plimsoll line of the poo, the brighter the flame. Less educational, but more hygienic, to flush first. Again, it's all a bit of a chore and the toilet then has that give-away stink of a burnt match.
  (**TIP**: Don't leave it floating in the pan, but don't put it still smouldering in the bin either.)

- Fresh Drop. A single drop of this 'magic smell eater' takes out even the worst culprits. It contains 'perfume, plant extracts, disinfectant, chemical deodorizer, surface active agent and alcohol' and I've no idea how it works. But it does. For best results, you put a drop in before you go, but if you want to wallow in your glory, it's still pretty effective if you add it afterwards.

What's the correct position for a poo?

Ideally, squatting so your hips are lower than your knees. The French drop-off holes may look a bit sparse, but they get the anatomy just right, allowing a natural unfurling of the sigmoid colon and rectum so the poo slides out with minimal encouragement. The low squat is also a great position for having a baby, particularly behind a bush.

As you get older and your hips stiffen, you may have difficulty getting up from a low toilet. Raising the seat can help, but then you may find the poo is less gratifying. One solution is a stool-stool, that allows you to raise your feet and hence knees to poo, then you can kick it away and slide off swiftly to light a match.

Should you stand up or sit down to wipe?

There is no moral imperative here, it's just a matter of personal choice, mobility and manual dexterity. There's more variation in arse-wiping than just about any sport. From the type of paper used, number of sheets selected, folded, scrunched-up or moistened. A sit-down wipe requires a point of access and a long arm going in blind, but your buttocks are spread nicely. Standing up is superficially easier but unsatisfying as the buttocks are clenched. So most people opt for a semi-squat, strongest foot forward, wiping front-to-back. Some analyse the wipings closely for blood, worms, contact lenses etc. Others can't wait to flush them away.

Posh people don't bother with any of this nonsense and head straight for the bidet. If space is cramped, you can even buy 'a toilet with bidet functionality' (**NOTE:** Read the instructions carefully). Those less fortunate make their own bidet with a shower head, either dangling precariously over the bath or squatting, but nearly always ending up with very wet pants. Some men don't even bother wiping and when they do, only half wash their hands afterwards.

Is it OK to rinse out a toilet brush in the sink?

Not in my sink. Toilet brushes are a terrible design. One minute you're earning brownie points by removing brownies from the pan, the next you've got a multi-bristled nylon monster covered in bits of shit. Hide it back in the container and you've lost all your brownie points. Wash it out in the sink and your bits flick all over the toothbrushes. If you're desperate, you could maybe use the bath if there's one to hand. Or just leave it in the pan to soak overnight in bleach, with a post it note on the door to remind yourself what you've done, so nobody sits on it in the middle of the night (uncomfortable if it's you, minus 1,000 brownie points if it's not).

Why are the British obsessed with their bowels?

The ruling classes have always wanted to rule their bowels too and, for centuries, tried to train them to be regular as clockwork, at the same time every morning. Matrons lined up small boys in public schools and forced syrup of figs down them. In the First World War, this bowel fixation spread along the trenches, from the officers to the foot soldiers, and we've never quite recovered, which is why we still waste a fortune on laxatives every year. What matters is not how often you go, but whether it slips out easily when you do. Fruit, fibre, fluid, a knees-up and a happy disposition are generally all you need.

Is Bristol proud of its Stool chart?

It certainly should be. The stool chart was developed by two Bristol doctors, Heaton and Lewis, who proposed you could tell how quickly food passed through your digestive tract by peering at your poo. Common sense would suggest that if you're passing liquid, it's racing through on the back of a vindaloo; if you're taking eons to squeeze out a solitary rabbit pellet, then you could do with the hurry-ups.

But common sense alone is not enough for scientists. They need proof. So Heaton and Lewis took sixty-six volunteers and measured their 'whole-gut transit time' with radiopaque marker pellets and weighed their stools, as well as keeping a diary of their form and frequency on a seven-point 'stool scale'. The transit time (i.e. the time for marker pellet to go from mouth to anus) was then altered with senna (speeds it up) and loperamide (slows it down), and the measurements were repeated. Surprise! There was a good correlation between the fluidity of the stool and how quickly it took to appear.

You can download the Bristol Stool Form Scale from the internet, and it makes a delightful, educational and cheap credit-crunch game to get you through the long holidays. Type 1 are separate hard lumps, like walnuts and as uncomfortable to pass. Type 2 are like a home-made or organic sausage and all bumpy. Type 3 is an easier, production-line sausage with cracks on the surface. Type 4 is a smooth, soft easily-coiled snake. Type 5 are soft Mr Blobbies with clear-cut edges, Type 6 are mushy, fluffy, raggedy-edged pieces. And Type 7 is the entirely-liquid-you-won't-be-going-far-today sort.

To make it more interesting, you can correlate what you eat and whether you wash your hands before meals, with your stool form. And for the real enthusiast on a rainy day, try check out the colour. Poo is usually brown because of the combination of iron and the pigment bilirubin in the bowel. But the shade of brown can vary enormously. Get a Dulux chart from B&Q and see if you can spot a hint of African Dawn or a touch of Moonlanding. Keep a diary and show it to your GP. I'm sure she'll be fascinated. For anyone with access to radiopaque marker pellets, you could study the form first, and then bet on how quickly you think it will take the next one to pass through.

NOTE: None of these puerile games are advocated by Heaton or Lewis in their serious research, published in the *Scandanavian Journal of Gastroenterology* (Volume 32, Issue 9, September 1997, pp. 920–24).

ANOTHER NOTE: Obvious red blood in the poo needs checking out, as does a very pale poo (could be down to jaundice) and a black one, especially if it really, really, really stinks. Meleana – the result of altered blood passing through the bowels – is both a domestic and medical emergency. Dial 999 and open the window.

Can farting spread disease?

Possibly. A study reported in the *New Scientist* of young men dropping their trousers and farting forcefully onto a Petri dish found that some germs were transmitted. The clinical significance of this is unclear – bugs normally get trapped in corduroy – but it's certainly unhelpful to fart loudly in someone's face, even without your trousers down (unless you're invited to).

Is farting always someone else's fault?

Sadly, we live in a blame culture. In families without a dog, a disproportionately large percentage of farts get blamed on the eldest male, which is one of the few advantages of having relatives over for Christmas. Healthy men let one go between 14 and 25 times a day and women half as often, although women occasionally produce a stronger smell.

In socially embarrassing situations (e.g. Midnight Mass), it's possible for those with good musculature to keep the sphincter tight but pressure always finds a way out, and some of the gas is absorbed through the gut wall, into the bloodstream and out via the lungs. So you really can speak out of your arse. Others, particularly the older relative and mother of four, are a bit slacker down below and find it impossible to hold on. As with comedy, the secret is timing. You'd be surprised what pops out in the chorus of 'Ding Dong Merrily on High'.

So, how does the wind get there? Every time we swallow, we gulp in air too and fizzy drinks compound this. Bicarbonate in the saliva and pancreatic juices react with stomach acid to produce carbon dioxide and many of our gut bacteria react with whatever's passing through to produce methane, hydrogen and more CO_2. All of these cause wind, but it's the tiny amount of sulphurous gas that make it smell.

Farting and belching in the absence of other symptoms are entirely healthy. Indeed, the Dutch Liver Foundation once launched a publicity campaign encouraging people to break wind fifteen times a day. A happy medium would be to go easy on food with a high proportion of unabsorbable carbohydrate, that provide a feeding frenzy for the lower gut bacteria. These include beans, peas, broccoli, cauliflower, Jerusalem artichokes, root vegetables, raisins, prunes, apples and fruit juice (which is heavy in fructose). You'll note that all of these are supposed to be very good for you, and wind is often the price you pay for a healthy diet.

A lot of slimming products contain sorbitol and fructose, and also cause wind. Slimming drugs that prevent the absorption of fat cause a bowel explosion if you continue eating it. Fizzy drinks, gulping, eating too fast and overeating stack up the gut with wind that will escape either up or down, as does smoking, chewing gum and sucking on pen tops. Tight clothing and 'hold it in' underwear give your bowel gas fewer options.

A brisk outdoor walk is a great way of reliving the pressure and a charcoal biscuit or tablet (available from pharmacies) can minimise the smell. Chemists have other anti-flatulence products and in extreme cases, Under-Tec pants have a carbon filter gusset or you can buy a cushion called a Flatulence Filter (with a tweed cover) to absorb the smell. Or simply put on a broad Australian accent, proclaim 'better out than in' and tuck into the sprouts.

When is it OK to relieve yourself in public?

It depends which culture you inhabit. In many countries, it's deemed acceptable for a line of male strangers to pee and glance together, but there's an unwritten etiquette that you space yourself out as far away as you can from any existing customers so you don't mark out another man's territory (or piss on his trousers).

Peeing in the street is an unpleasant side effect of very cheap alcohol and a faulty 'I've had enough button'. Eight pints go in and ten come out. There's a risk of an indecent exposure charge for adults, particularly now there are security cameras on every corner, but convictions are rare. Pooing in front of strangers remains a huge taboo. Close family, rugby tours and confused patients aside, I've only observed two adults pooing in the flesh, both on a Westcoast Virgin explorer. The toilet doors on the new trains are so complicated, you need a physics degree to lock them. Many users inadvertently leave the lock sign flashing, which isn't locked at all. As a result, I've surprised two fellow travellers and I only use the service occasionally, so God knows how many others have been caught with their trousers down. The natural reaction is to leap up and hit the close button, but it's a good few paces away and then the door takes a good five seconds to shut. It would be hard to design a more effective ritual humiliation.

Interestingly, the toilet on the Trans-Pennine Express I've just used has a similar sliding door, but a far more obvious flip-switch locking mechanism, so it can be done. If you'd like to join the Virgin Explorer Toilet Survivors Club (VET-SUC) we meet every first Monday in the bar of the Ring of Bells. There are separate entrances for the doers and the viewers, to allow time for mutual recognition before closure is achieved by a brief shake of the hands (washed first, of course).

Forty per cent of the world's population have it even worse than a VET-SUC doer. They've got no safe place to poo or flush. In the UK, going outdoors is frowned upon because of the public health risk, but in many countries, pooing outdoors is entirely normal because there's no alternative. The charity Wateraid recently 'raised public awareness' of this by filming four volunteers doing very realistic fake poos on the pavements of London and posting them on YouTube. As Charlotte, who played the role of a traffic warden caught short while ticketing cars, put it: 'I know it may look funny, but I felt really exposed.' Ah, the things you do when you're resting between jobs.

In the UK, the Sanitation Bill, passed in 1848, has done far more for the health of the nation than the founding of the NHS a century later, but it's good to be reminded how lucky we are. 2.6 billion people in the world do not have access to adequate sanitation and it kills 5,000 children every day. A single gram of human faeces weighs in with 10,000,000 viruses, 1,000,000 bacteria, 1,000 parasite cysts and 100 parasite eggs. Hardly surprising then that water-related disease is the world's second biggest killer. If we lived in a country where a good dose of dysentery was the price to pay for poor personal hygiene, then even doctors would wash their hands properly. If you want to witness a mock poo, search YouTube for 'pooing in public'. Please try not to laugh or get sexually aroused. If you just want to donate to WaterAid, go to www.wateraid.org/uk/. Now wash your hands.

If it moves, is it rude?

Wobbling was the Lord Chamberlain's criterion for the difference between art and obscenity. When flesh appeared on stage at Soho's Windmill theatre, one dancer famously managed to hold it together during a bombing raid, but then freaked obscenely a few days later when she spied a mouse. When the Lord Chamberlain's office shut up shop in the late sixties, there was a moving-flesh explosion: *Hair, Oh Calcutta, Let My People Come* and all the strip bars.

Anything curved looks ruder when it moves because it suggests both action and friction. I thought the criterion had died out with the good Lord until I made a programme about erectile dysfunction for the BBC, with the help of a heroic nurse specialist called Nolly Biggins. Sister Biggins was carefully demonstrating the injection of a rubber penis with a hardening drug called Caverjet, a sequence we'd cleared with the BBC Thought Police for pre-watershed viewing. Alas, in the edit suite the penis was noted to have 'wobbled offensively' and couldn't be aired.

If a woman starts periods at the menarche, when does a man start ejaculating?

At the ejacularche. The term was coined by Israeli and Scandinavian sexologists, but has yet to enter popular usage. 'Look at these snail tracks on the duvet. Malcolm must have passed the ejacularche.'

How do I choose which size sanitary towels to buy my partner?

Tough call. We all want to be new, or rather 'reconstructed', men and what could be more thoughtful than clicking on female hygiene when you're shopping online or hiding tampons at the bottom of a bulging basket? But what should you buy? The comic Ian Cognito did a great routine about panty liners: 'Why the hell have they got wings? I'd have thought the last thing you want on a panty liner is wings. Sudden gust of wind and over you go.'

There is no solution to the sanitary confusion, other than to ask your partner what she wants. If you guess, you'll never get it right and you risk a terrible row. Never, under any circumstances, try to surprise her with Extra Heavy-Duty All-Night Cling-On Maxi Towels, even if you've found them in the Tesco Favourites list. Each one is roughly the size of a sheep. She'll never forgive you for knowing.

Why do women clean up when men pee all over the floor?

I don't know. Studies have shown that if men do their fair share of toilet cleaning, they make far less mess. I know one woman who, whenever her partner pees on the toilet seat, pees on his car seat. He still hasn't twigged after sixteen years.

Why does it hurt when I pee?

This question, from the back of a theatre in Canterbury, was thrown at me wrapped round a urine sample (dark, smelly yellow in a proper sample pot with the lid tightly screwed on). 'PS: Stings like buggery and can't get an appointment. Please help.' And why not? I tasted (sorry, tested) the pee on stage and it had blood, white cells and cranberry juice in it. For a second opinion, I tossed it to a local GP in the front row. Lots of women come to comedy gigs with urine infections but not many leave with a prescription for antibiotics. Not terribly ethical but better than spending the weekend pissing razor blades.

'Why does it hurt when I pee?' is also a seminal song from Frank

Zappa's 1979 rock opera *Joe's Garage*. It includes the mighty fine rhyme:

> **My balls feel like a pair of maracas**
> **Oh God I've probably got the gono-coc-coc-coccus**

Which is almost as good as his more famous couplet:

> **Watch out where the huskies go**
> **and don't you eat that yellow snow**

The character with painful pee is Joe, whose attempts to become a rock star have been diverted by a liaison with a lady at the taco stand. Being a bloke, Joe doesn't use a condom and doesn't want to admit he might have a dose, preferring to ascribe his symptoms to something he caught from the toilet seat. He doesn't want a doctor to stick a needle (or an umbrella) in him, but the good news is that treatment has come on in leaps and bounds since 1979. There are no umbrellas and often no swabs these days. Just a urine sample and some tablets.

Frank Zappa can be a bit impenetrable (his children are Moon Unit, Dweezil, Ahmet Emuukha Rodan and Diva Thin Muffin Pigeen), but *Joe's Garage* is a fine album. Zappa narrates as the Central Scrutinizer, whose job it is to enforce all the laws that haven't yet been passed. The opera satirizes sex, the music business, McCarthyism, censorship and Scientology, and it flips my mood into something more mischievous. Zappa, alas, ceased being mischievous at just 53. He died from prostate cancer or, as his family put it, he 'left for his final tour just before 6pm on Saturday' (4 December 1993).

Back on Earth, it hurts when we pee because we've evolved pain receptors along our urinary tract to tell us when something isn't quite right. Either that, or God decided to create them for you on a quiet day. ('I know, I'll line the mammalian urinary tract with pain receptors. But first, I'll design an orchid that looks like the sexual parts of a bee.')

Either way, anything that inflames the bladder or urethra makes it hurt when you pee. Could be a urine infection from bugs in the bowel, a urethral infection in bugs from someone else's urethra or bowel, the remains of a kidney stone, or a misplaced pipe cleaner. All of these can be treated if you conquer your embarrassment. Just highlight this section and show it to the receptionist. She'll understand.

Women tend to get more urine infections than men because the wee hole is closer to the poo hole (or at least it should be), and it's easy to forget to wipe front-to-back (especially when hovering above the nettles on the hard shoulder). If you've survived the menopause, a bit of oestrogen cream can do wonders down below. It's not easy discussing vaginal dryness with a GP and some of the drug names don't make a trip to the chemist that comfortable either: 'I'm here for my Vagifem.' Get out the highlighter pen again.

Dehydration can occasionally make the urine sting and is easily sorted, but sometimes we really don't know why it hurts so we mask our ignorance with a silly name like 'interstitial cystitis' or 'urethral syndrome'. Any pain that's accompanied by pus needs to be shared with a doctor urgently (and before you share it with anyone else).

And let's not forget guilt as a cause of painful pee. Consultations in a sexual health clinic often start with something like 'I was away at a conference/beach holiday/cider festival', middling with 'seven bottles of Thatchers' and climaxing with 'not sure what we did but it didn't include a condom.' Usually the guilt kicks in before any symptoms, and people bring it along to the clinic in the hope of absolution and a clean bill of health.

'Not wanting to pass anything on to my partner' often goes hand in hand with 'Not wanting to tell my partner', but for those who choose an HIV test, it needs to be done (or repeated) twelve weeks after the risky sex, during which time you're advised not to have any more sex. A three month lay-off can be hard to explain to your partner unless you develop the mother of all migraines or 'accidentally' catch your foreskin in your zip . . . repeatedly.

But even when every test for every infection has come back negative, some people still have the symptoms of an infection, as the brain comes to terms with the guilty secret. Pleasure needs a light muzzle, or at the very least a condom. And two minutes of gooey mess doesn't always equate with long-term contentment.

4

Surreal sex guide

FLYING SOLO

Is wanking a form of genocide?

No. Young men offload hundreds of millions of sperm, just for fun, on most days of the year. The comedian Bill Hicks pondered the lost civilisations wasted on his stomach but the good news is that, although women are born with all their eggs, the sperm factory stays in production until the day you die. So your losses are always replaced and there's no need to feel profligate. Most sperm never get anywhere near an egg, even when you're trying to make a baby.

Do love eggs need to be fitted?

No. They come in a variety of sizes and materials, so it's a case of suck it and see. Most are roughly spherical, either metal, silicone, rubber or plastic, and of varying diameters. If you're shopping abroad, they may be sold as Ben-Wa balls, geisha balls, Burmese bells, Thai beads, Ri-no-tama or Mien-Ling. Older versions are balls within balls, with a drop of mercury to aid wiggling or a sliver tongue that vibrates. All are inserted into the vagina (not all at once) and are said to produce pleasurable sensations on running for the bus.

Individual experimentation is needed to determine which are most likely to make you miss the bus, which are best for your pelvic floor, and which can be heard by small children and Labradors. But the fact that love eggs have existed in so many cultures for centuries suggest there must be something in them (other than mercury).

Newer, high-tech love eggs are more bullet-shaped (typically three inches by three quarters of an inch) and slip easily into (but less easily out of) the vagina and anus. If an adults-only egg hunt sounds too much of a fiddle, you can get eggs connected to a wire and control panel that allows various modes of electrical vibration (the forward surge or the side-to-side shuffle, or a mixture of the two at varying speeds). The wire aids retrieval but makes covert use on the bus more of a challenge.

Top of the range are the battery eggs that can be controlled remotely using wireless technology. This allows you a whole range of pleasurable sensations whilst pretending to play Nintendo on the top deck. You can also buy sleeves for your eggs with 'textural nubs and ribs' for added pleasure. Then there's the infamous double-yolker, to satisfy the heartiest of appetites. So why not go to work on an egg?

NOTE: A lost love egg is not quite a medical emergency, and may not get the priority you feel it deserves during a flu pandemic. To avoid embarrassment, always buy eggs with strings attached, rather than free-range.

Do voice activated vibrators work?

Not very well, judging by the number of them in the Christmas sales. The trouble with VAVs is that most people train them to work with their normal voice, which is a completely different pitch, intonation and even language from their masturbation voice. If, on the other hand, you train your VAV to understand your 'unique pleasure tones', you'll find that all sorts of things will set it off (the Hoover, the children squabbling, an egg whisk, a hungry pony). Most vibrators are complicated enough (three heads, four fingers, five speeds, iPod docking port, sat nav for the clitoris). Voice activation is unnecessary icing on the cock.

Do people who work from home masturbate more?

Almost certainly. It's known as hot-desking. The relationship between self-pleasure at work and its effect on productivity is unclear. There seems to be a delicate balance between reducing stress and frustration on the one hand, and dozing off afterwards or having to call out the keyboard engineer, on the other. But the overall effect appears to be positive. How long before we see wank stations next to the water cooler?

How do you stop a teenage boy wanking all the time?

Don't. Adolescence is tough enough without losing your principle pleasure. And never burst in trying to catch him mid-wank. It's even more psychologically damaging than waking a sleepwalker. Privacy is important once the hormones kick in. Knock loudly, count to ten elephants and only enter if summoned. 'Just a minute' generally means just that.

Masturbation is entirely healthy within the constraints of the culture you're living in (don't do it in public, do try to get at least some of your homework done first). It helps develop the imagination and should be the cheapest guilt-free fun anyone can have. Many boys (and men) find their dominant hand runs a shuttle service between knob and nose during the waking hours, and if it's causing difficulties during, say, a dental examination, use an enigmatic code word to break him out of his reverie. In a recent *Sunday Times* survey, the top three scratch-and-sniff breakers were 'orchid', 'avocado' and 'flange.'

Who invented masturbatory guilt?

Masturbatory guilt goes back at least to the Middle Ages, and continues today for those who've been poorly parented or got in with the wrong church. Degeneracy theory held that all diseases were due to the loss of semen and some other vital fluid, and that demons collected the semen from masturbatory and nocturnal emissions, and used it to create new bodies for themselves. But as any teenage boy knows, not even the Devil cleans up after you and the only way to hide the mess is to use a wank sock or wipe it on the curtains.

The semen-demon theory took a bit of a pounding in the seventeenth and eighteenth centuries, as science tried to fight back. Then in the 1750s, up popped Swiss doctor Simon Tissot who was convinced that every disease (even in women) and death itself were related to the unnecessary spillage of intimate secretions. Women's secretions were apparently 'less valuable and less matured' than their male equivalent, but could still kill women if they indulged in excessive sex, particularly of the type that 'sent them into spasm'.

John Harvey Kellogg may have invented that golden flake of corn but for a doctor, he had a shockingly regressive view of masturbation. Circumcision without anaesthetic was advocated for boys caught having a fiddle: 'The brief pain attending the operation will have a salutary effect upon the mind, especially if it be connected with the idea of punishment, as it may well be in some cases. The soreness which continues for several weeks interrupts the practice, and if it had not previously become too firmly fixed, it may be forgotten and not resumed.' Girls and women caught touching their genitals fared little better: 'The application of pure carbolic acid to the clitoris an excellent means of allaying the abnormal excitement.' Dr Kellogg died in 1943, aged ninety-one, without once ever masturbating. Yeah, right.

In 1924, *Harmsworth's Home Doctor* remained to be convinced about the benefits of self-pleasure:

> *Masturbation is the most prevalent of all sexual disorders. It is very commonly found in the mentally unstable, the insane and sexual perverts, but it is not the fact that masturbation in an otherwise normal individual can produce idiocy [that's me and Dr Harmsworth off the hook then]. In the earliest years of life, the condition is often started by the presence of some irritative condition of the genital organs which leads to the child scratching itself, and the relief obtained leads to the continuance of the bad habit . . . Occasionally ignorant and irresponsible nursemaids are in the habit of soothing irritable and crying children by manipulation of the genitals, and the child rapidly acquires the habit as it gives rise to pleasurable sensations.*

And there's more.

*In older children who are at school, certain
physical exercises necessitating the rubbing
of the thighs together may actually start the
condition; often, however, the child is taught the
habit by some older boy or girl in the school who is
addicted to it. Treatment is by the encouragement
of outdoor pursuits. The child should be watched
specially, but no retaining apparatus should be
worn to prevent the habit.*

At least Dr Harmsworth seems a lot kinder than Dr Kellog and
gives a rosy prognosis for most of us:

*It is true that erotic practice on the self is breaking a
biological law and may lead to many mental warps.
However, in the majority of cases, psychotherapy in
proper hands [sic], with true knowledge of all that is
involved will not fail to put matters right.*

If you don't masturbate, doesn't it just come out at night?

If you're young or very abstemious, yes. The famous sexologist
Alfred Kinsey found that ninety per cent of men and forty per
cent of women had experienced nocturnal orgasms. You'd think
that might get you off the hook but authority has been hard
on wet dreams as far back as the Bible. Deuteronomy (23:10)
recommended that sheet-stainers be sent home from camp:
'If there be among you any man, that is not clean by reason of
uncleanness that chanceth him by night, then shall he go abroad
out of the camp, he shall not come within the camp.'

Leviticus (15:16–18) was equally tough however the emission
occurred. 'And if a man has an emission of semen, he shall bathe his

whole body in water, and be unclean until the evening. If a man lies with a woman and has an emission of semen, both of them shall bathe themselves in water and be unclean until the evening.'

There's absolutely nothing unclean about semen, unless you've got an infection. Wiping it all over your belly is a lot easier than changing the sheets. It can stick hairs together and make back-combing a challenge, but you don't need to wash it off immediately with water unless you get it in your eye.

Is it normal to make a racket when you're on your own?

Yes, yes, yes. If you're interested in the extraordinary variety of sound and vision emanating from ordinary people masturbating, check out the Beautiful Agony website. It only shows faces, but they're by far the most interesting part of the body. A wonderful guilt-free, pleasure-affirming site.

Is masturbation ever harmful?

Yes. If you're in a relationship and you do it to the exclusion of other forms of intimacy, you may find the relationship doesn't last long. And if you do it with a noose around your neck for the extra rush of asphyxia, you may not last long either. Never gasp alone, no matter how good your quick-release knots are. Find a very understanding partner with advanced resuscitation skills.

VERY BASIC INSTINCTS

Has everyone had more sex than me?

No. Virginity and abstinence are very fashionable, and negative sex can be emotional or physical, but not numerical. So relax, love yourself and check out the fabulous 'Everyone Else Has Had More Sex Than Me' video on YouTube. The song is by the Melbourne-based band TISM (This Is Serious Mum), and the animation by Bernard Derriman features a procession of bunnies with numbers on their shirts corresponding to how many times they've had sex. The sexiest rabbit by far is the singer (number one). Number zero (on keyboards) could be equally attractive but he or she is wearing a mask. This is not to suggest that all virgins should cover up, but a nod to the TISM quirk of always wearing masks in public (and perhaps during sex).

Is it OK to be not terribly interested in sex?

Absolutely. Sex with the same person gets a bit samey no matter how many manuals you read, and when all the bits start dangling down and drying up, it can be quite a fiddle trying to fit them together again. We don't know how often people have sex because it's all done by survey, rather than a two-way mirror, and there's a tendency to round up to something impressive. But some couples say they have sex once or twice a year and are perfectly happy. Losing your libido with age leaves time for new hobbies. Why thrash about like a grounded mackerel when you could be spraying the roses? It only becomes a ball-breaker if one of you wants more (not always the man) and isn't happy tugging away like a teenager.

The male sexual response is fairly basic. When you're young, it's like a traffic light stuck on green. As you get older, a bit of amber creeps in which can fairly easily be tickled into green. A lot of green men will take sex if it's offered to them, even if it's not terribly wise and they don't have a condom. Every man gets an occasional red, particularly if you're tired, stressed, pissed or low. If you get stuck on red, you can either get help or give up and make chutney. Young women tend to start life on amber but can appear to go green without wanting penetrative sex. Outside certain S&M games, 'no' always means 'no'.

As women get older, and particularly if they've had children, they trade up their consent-to-sex system for something that wouldn't look out of place in the cockpit of a stealth bomber. There are dozens of dials that all have to be in exactly the right position for take off: family fed, dog fed, cat fed, rubbish out, fridge mended, washing done, washing-up done, toilets cleaned, house vacuumed, book finished, children's homework done, holiday planned, tomorrow's meals planned, mother phoned, period finished, sleep caught up on, back too sore, hot bath, back just about OK, clean sheets, non-farty-smelling bedroom, phone off the hook, check the kids are asleep, diligent and detailed foreplay, condom checked, stop, condom checked again, stop, 'I'm sure I heard the kids', check the kids again, ten minutes explaining what a condom is and what it's doing on the penis poking out of your dressing gown, bribe kids to pretend to be asleep for ten minutes, creep back, wake wife up, start again, stop, are you sure you've put the cat out? . . . and enjoy.

If you're a bloke, there are two options. You can help her with that mountain of tedious household chores you take for granted when you don't want sex, in the hope that she won't use the window of opportunity you've skilfully created to watch *Desperate Housewives*. Or you can slope off for a tug. As I said, sex isn't everything.

Remember too that there are times in a relationship when you'd be foolish to expect too much sex. These include:

- **After childbirth**
- **During childbirth**
- **During a cycling holiday**
- **While moving house**

- **When your partner's asleep**
- **When the cat's died**

Sexual advances in mid-marriage hinge on the delicate combination of timing and mind-reading. 'I'm going upstairs for a lie down' could mean 'come and join me, tiger' or, more likely, 'I'm going upstairs for a lie down.' If you have trouble judging each other's mood, a secret sign works wonders. Marmite on the top shelf, game on. Marmite on the bottom shelf, no chance.

NOTE: The Marmite sign will fail if someone in the house actually eats the stuff and puts it back on the opposite shelf or, even more confusing, the middle shelf. It will also fail if your kids twig why you've kept an unopened jar of Marmite in the pantry for sixteen years, and then mess with your mind by putting it in the fridge. Bastards.

Is it normal to laugh during sex?

Yes. Laughter (preferably mutual) is one of the principal pleasures of sex unless you're trying to make a baby, in which case it's terribly serious and we must do it now. If you just want to have an orgasm, you can always sort yourself out (and you're far more likely to succeed). If you want a good belly laugh too, let your bellies slap together like the waves against the shore. Then look at each other closely and try to hold it together. Sex faces are priceless. If your partner doesn't get it, hold a mirror up when he's working up to the vinegar strokes. Mr Tomato Head does *The Scream*. This is, incidentally, an excellent cure for premature ejaculation and far easier to execute than the squeeze technique.

Nature has helpfully provided us with the sights, sounds and smells to make sex far more rewarding than your average comedy gig. You may have put a half-cooked sausage in your mouth before, but not with two hairy teabags hanging off your chin. Whoever came up with that? Then there are the fanny farts, the pubes in teeth, the missed entry, the absurdly loud groans and the slurping of moist membranes being rubbed together.

A lot of people find it hard to tell a joke, but ask anyone to talk dirty to you and you'll be on the floor. 'Fill me with your man milk, you ginger love stud.' 'Grip me with those luscious love lips, you horny harlot.' Even better, try dirty talk with correct anatomical terms: 'Keep that *pubococcygeus* nice and taut,' 'Take me with your *tunica albuginea*,' and 'Sit on my face and show me your vestibule.'

Sex works best when you do things together (laugh, move, breathe . . .). It becomes a problem when only one of you does it. If your partner stops breathing altogether, the heart's probably stopped too and you have to try to restart it. Quickly. *(see* **What do I do if someone dies on me during sex?**) Otherwise, most people's sex lives are vastly improved by slowing down and not taking it too seriously. Start by comparing hoods. At least then you'll both know where the clitoris is.

Is comedy just sex in disguise?

Sex is a continuation of comedy. A lot of couples go to comedy gigs as a less taxing alternative to foreplay. You laugh, you loosen up, you go home and shag (not terribly successfully if you've overdone the pear cider). And women rate sense of humour so highly because when sex doesn't go quite as planned, there's nothing worse than being stuck under the covers with someone who doesn't see the funny side and just carries on plugging away earnestly in the hope it'll come good.

The funniest comedians are the ones you see for the first time. Go back the following week and, even if they claim most of the set is improvised, you start to spot patterns and punchlines coming. It can still be funny, but less laugh-out-loud; more cosy recognition. But if you see the same comedian every week for twenty years and he does pretty much the same routine, you start wondering if you should heckle or ask for your money back. But you're too shy to do that, so you go off and read a book instead. Or maybe go and see another comedian.

Most people in long-term relationships have sex in much the same way every time (except maybe at the beginning, when you risk asking for something a bit kinky before the pattern is set, and you can still get away with 'everybody else does it'). After a few months, you can predict how it's going to go. Right tit, left tit, quick lick, your turn, stick your tongue out, fire. 'Ooh, I wasn't expecting that.' 'Sorry, I'll get you a tissue.'

Some people use comedy or sex to get rid of aggression, but it rarely results in mutual pleasure or laughter. The best communication unites, rather than divides, and surprises without causing harm. Most people have two jokes and two sexual positions in them, none of which they've mastered particularly well and certainly not standing up in front of an audience. But it's amazing what a bit of practice can achieve. **TIP:** If you explain a joke to a silent audience, you will die. If you explain a sexual manoeuvre to a silent partner you will provoke gales of laughter. 'I'm just kneading your breasts and now I'm going to plait them.'

How soon can I have sex after a heart attack?

Assuming you survive the heart attack, you can attempt sex again as soon as you feel up to it. This is generally anything from a few weeks onwards. As the British Heart Foundation (BHF) puts it: 'It is usually fine to have sex if you can climb two flights of stairs briskly without getting chest discomfort or becoming breathless.' That's half the population stuffed then.

As for which position to adopt out of your vast armory of

two, I'd kick off in bed, rather than silly mid-off on the stairs, and with the one where your partner does most of the work, The BHF also suggest that you don't have a heavy meal or too much booze beforehand, you keep the room warm, avoid cold sheets and choose a relaxing atmosphere. Fifty pence says you'll be asleep in two minutes.

It's also worth having a secret sign for a time-out and your GTN spray at the ready, in case you get a twinge of chest pain. Sex, like any exercise, is very good for you whether you've had a heart attack or not. If you've had surgery, it's worth avoiding any heavy chest action that might put a strain on the scar. And remember there's plenty you can do with your hands if you don't fancy the full two-minute body squelch.

How soon can I have sex after the cat's died?

Again, there's no strict guidance here, but assuming your partner is more upset than you are over the loss of the family pet, she/ he may well need your support and consolation. A needy hug should not, under any circumstances, be taken as a come on. A healthy grieving process can go through shock, anger, numbness and denial but ends with acceptance. As soon as the litter tray and the cat biscuits are packed away, you could perhaps make some tentative enquiries. But go easy. And avoid cold sheets. If you're really brave, you could suggest: 'It's what Tipsy would have wanted,' but it could go either way. A safer alternative is to bring out the Marmite *(see* **Is it OK to be not terribly interested in sex?**)

Is infidelity normal?

Depends what you mean by normal. It certainly appears to be quite common, so far as people will admit to it (anonymously, obviously). The National Survey of Sexual Attitudes and Lifestyles is a ten-yearly UK survey of over 11,000 Brits aged between sixteen and forty-four. Why they stop at forty-four I've no idea, since many people have their best sex when the kids have left home. The last study found that, in the year 2000, 9 per cent of women and 14.6 per cent of men had 'more than one partner at the same time'. This could be taken both ways, but I imagine that's pretty rare. Even the 'former millionaire shagging machine' Frank Skinner has only ever had one threesome: 'I spent the whole thing feeling terribly self-conscious. What were they whispering?' Skinner is an extraordinarily open, observational comic. He once came across a piece of errant tissue paper during oral sex 'like a cloakroom ticket tucked behind a lapel'.

Most people squeeze in extra sex as secretly as they can, dogs permitting, and the best guess is that in fifty per cent of all couples, one (or both) partners will have strayed at least once. The question is not so much is it normal, but is it worth it?

The survey is due to be repeated in 2010, so it'll be interesting to see how we've all been behaving over the last decade. Ten years ago, the 'mean number of lifetime partners' (as opposed to the number of mean lifetime partners) was 12.7 for men and 6.5 for women. Leaving aside the challenge of having sex with 0.5 of a person, it suggests that either men are having more sex with men or that men exaggerate and women downsize. Or perhaps some people just aren't very good at counting or spotting when they've changed partners. **TIP:** Look at the face.

Other millennium highlights include:

- **Average age for first intercourse was seventeen for women and sixteen for men.**

- **The proportion of men in Britain who had ever had a homosexual partner was 5.4 per cent**

- **12.3 per cent of men and 11.3 per cent of women**

had tried anal sex that year (but not for the whole year).

- 10.1 per cent of women and 15.4 per cent of men had risky sex as defined as 'two or more heterosexual and/or homosexual partners in the last year and inconsistent condom use.'

- 1 in 5 men and 1 in 4 women had stuck to one sexual partner so far.

- On average across the UK, 1 in 23 men had paid for sex. In London, 1 in 11 men had.

- 1 in 10 of those surveyed knew they'd had at least one sexually transmitted infection, with Chlamydia being the most common. The number who didn't know they had a dose is unknown, but is likely to be substantial since the commonest symptom is no symptoms at all.

Is marriage really good for your health?

Yes, but only if you stay married. You may be better off never having married, rather than separated by divorce or death. Generally speaking . . .

- Both women and men live longer and remain healthier in happy marriages. Men also live longer in unhappy marriages (presumably because women still wipe the piss up).

- Traumatic separation is expensive (financially, psychologically, socially and physically). The divorced or widowed are more likely to get depressed in the aftermath, and also to get cancer, heart disease, diabetes, dementia and mobility problems further down the line. In some marriages, people get so reliant on each other that they don't cope well alone.

- Marriages are not automatically happy, but neither is living apart. Rather like cosmetic enhancement, some people go through a lot of separation pain to find themselves even more dissatisfied (and a lot poorer) than when they started. Others relish their new freedom, at least until the money runs out.

- Marriages tend to last longer if you give each other space and don't turn over every stone or analyze every issue in tedious detail.

- Kids tend to do better at school if their parents stick together (unless they're being tortured).

- If you're divorced, you're less likely to get help and support from your children as you get older, and stepchildren rarely step in.

- Second marriages fail more frequently than first ones (unless you've managed to escape from a disastrous, abusive hell-hole).

None of this cuts much ice if you can't stand the sight, sound and smell of your partner anymore. All marriages need the warmth of a slow burn after the towering inferno has fizzled out. They also need a long-term vision, or some shared story of future contentment, particularly if the present is looking a bit grim. But if the present is looking very exciting thanks to the prolonged eye contact of that person over there, it takes a strong will to get out the 'stand to lose' checklist.

The health effects of infidelity haven't been widely studied, and seem to be very variable. If it goes badly, you end up with guilt and Chlamydia, one of which is far easier to sort than the other. If it goes very badly, you get rumbled and the walls come tumbling down (but can be rebuilt if there's a will).

On the plus side, there are people who appear to have very rewarding additional relationships, ranging from discrete 'fuck buddies' to those who love two people at the same time. The idea that there is one true love out there for each of us is clearly bollocks – there are loads of people we could have happy and content lives with – but to try to have them all at the same time seems a bit greedy.

There are lots of proposed causes of (excuses for) infidelity, ranging from selfish genes, poor or absent parenting, sex addiction and – my favourite – 'a regulatory emotional strategy for people with an avoidant-attachment disorder to release them from commitment phobia.' But the bottom line is that it's both a choice and a gamble. And as with all gambling, you should only risk what you're prepared to lose. Graciously.

Should I write an infidelity blog?

Humans are gossips, and if your affair is going swimmingly, you want to boast to someone about how happy/thin/breathless/ energized/peachy-skinned/fulfilled/less grumpy with the family it's making you feel. But you can't tell anyone you know. Because humans are gossips.

One solution is to write an infidelity blog. Men generally don't – they might boast via a brief e-mail or text to their mates (with photo attachment), but few can be arsed to knock off 800 words a day seeking the support and affirmation of strangers. But some women find it very therapeutic. Truewifeconfessions.blogspot. com sounds like the gateway to a porn site, but was founded by a woman called Dawn Rouse to allow women to 'say the unsayable'. Dawn is responsible for the first twenty confessions including: 'I know where your belt, glasses and wallet are. I just think it's funny to watch you run round like a crazy person looking for them' and 'Sometimes you only have to make me laugh to change my mood. It is not a strategy you use enough.'

The last thing these confessions are is 'unsayable'. Tell the poor bastard where his wallet is and then he'll reward you with a joke. Even better, make 'hunt the wallet' into a mild S&M game full of emotionally invigorating rewards and punishments (preferably involving the belt and spectacles).

There are a lot of infidelity blogs about, ranging from 'oh my gawd, I nearly got rumbled when his semen dripped down my leg during the school play' to cerebral reflection and poetry. A lot are about working through guilt. Most affairs get found out by something trivial: a loose hair, an errant earring, a pocketed receipt, a poorly timed text or a puddle under your seat at the school play. So it's quite a challenge to have an affair and blog about it every day, while deleting all traces of both. Having your cock and eating it. And not quite so affirming if it's read out in court. Still, there's some evidence that writing and reflecting on your life helps you cope with it better. And it's a lot cheaper than therapy. So put your best non-judgmental hat on and sample the sites below:

Yummymummyontheedge.blogspot.com

marriedwifeblog.blogspot.com

insidetheaffair.blogspot.com

serialmistress.blogspot.com

msscarlettletter.blogspot.com

Is watching porn a type of adultery?

Ask your partner. Some people are content for their partners to burn off excess energy watching strangers act very badly with no clothes on, others find any fantasy involving other people unacceptable (at least when it's not secretly hidden inside a brain). And, of course, it depends on the type of porn you're watching.

All porn can lead to 'pornification' – unrealistic expectations of the anatomy and behaviour of your partner. And if you find yourself whispering sweet nothings like 'what brings you to California?', 'call that a penis?' or 'I only popped in to fix the boiler,' then you probably should cancel your subscription.

You can't tell by watching porn who's performing willingly as a career move, who's fallen on hard times, who's desperate for the next fix and who's desperate to escape. Some sites are hallmarked to 'guarantee' everyone's over-age and giving of their time willingly, but the number of porn participants who end up with a leaky anus or HIV suggests it's not all fun, fun, fun.

In my home city, there's a porn production company that allows you (for a fee) to walk around the set, watch the filming and – for a birthday treat – appear as an extra. It makes a change from a balloon ride, but the view is far less impressive. As Kinglsey Amis observed, any genitals, when viewed sufficiently close, look like the inside of a giraffe's ear.

The most instructive and erotic site out there is Beautiful Agony. Based in Melbourne, it shows the faces of dozens of ordinary people coming. Not all in Australian accents. And volunteers film themselves, so there's none of that 'what brings you to Wagga Wagga?' nonsense.

The camera fixes solely on the face while a vast gallery of men and women sort themselves out. Some are screamingly funny, some just screaming and some very erotic. Some could be faking it, others putting it on for the camera, but there's little doubt that the face is where all the best action is. All you need is to be naked from the neck up.

The site is subtitled *'facettes de la petite mort'*, a reference to the near-death experience that the French, and others, have after orgasm. Of course, you can have a real death experience too, and not just from a heart attack. I once saw the comic Jack Dee lose his thread of thought on stage: 'I hate it when that happens. It's like when you're having sex with your wife and you run out of people to fantasise about.' There was a collective gasp followed by very loud laughter of recognition.

Does everyone else do it?

No. Suggestions one partner makes to another to fulfill a life-long fantasy (or after watching porn) are often followed up by the 'everybody else does it' line. Everybody else doesn't do it and, even if they did, all that matters is whether you want to do it. Talk it through. Don't be afraid to say 'no'. And if you try it, agree some ground rules and get-out clauses. Slowly, gently, safely, amusingly.

What's the difference between a prostitute and a sex worker?

Nothing, other than the reminder that sex workers should have defined rights, safety and protection like any other workers. In New Zealand, prostitution was decriminalised in 2003, when a reform act gave sex workers legal rights to help keep them (and their clients) safe. Indeed, sex work in NZ sounds as if its been given some thought:

- **You have the right to refuse to have sex with a client for any reason, or for no reason. You can't be fined for refusing to have sex either. And any person who tries to coerce you into sex commits an offence liable to imprisonment of up to fourteen years.**

- Local councils decide your place of work. Some allow work from home, others have zoned areas for brothels. Up to four sex workers can set up together without a licence, provided no one is boss. As soon as a manager is involved, you need a council licence. You don't have to register with the police.

- Managers, clients and sex workers must take all reasonable steps to ensure a condom or dental dam is used for vaginal, anal or oral sex.

- If you wish to leave sex work at any time, you can get benefit without any penalty imposed for voluntary unemployment.

- If you're a manager, client or newspaper publisher, you can be fined or imprisoned if you hire or advertise a sex worker who is under eighteen. It's also illegal to receive money from a sex worker under the age of eighteen (but not illegal to be a sex worker younger than eighteen).

Similar laws could be introduced in the UK but we don't talk about sex, much less about paying for it, so we haven't got round to decriminalising prostitution or protecting women generally. 200 women a year are murdered in the UK and the rape conviction rate is pitiful. Society should protect the most vulnerable, yet those sex workers who need the protection most (desperate for money, don't want to do it and driven out onto the street) are least likely to get it. The flip side is that commercial sex workers with their own premises have far more control and offer far safer sex than getting off with someone in a club and having a drunken, condomless fumble.

Five per cent of men pay for sex each year, and always will (though not necessarily the same five per cent). Women who want to be sex workers need employment rights, women who don't need protection and opportunity. You don't get either by criminalising both. And once you've taken all the steps you can to ensure sex between adults is consensual, where's the crime? Why not sign the petition at www.petitiononline.com/swsafety/petition.html? I'm number 1,578.

SEX IN NO PARTICULAR ORDER

How many different types of orgasm are there?

Men tend to classify orgasms according to how much comes out and whether they can hit the ceiling, but the intensity varies too (from a bit disappointing all the way up to those rare Tantric love gods who claim to be able to give themselves multiple orgasms by holding on forever). The pleasure is further diminished by infection – ejaculation may not be painful but if the sensation is just not right, you need a check-up (and especially if there's a big blob of pus on your pants before you've even started).

Women's orgasms, on the other hand, have been classified and labelled as you might a rare bird. You start with clitoral and vaginal, and then build up to tenting and A-frame and, if you're really lucky, blended. Tenting is triggered by clitoral stimulation (**TIP**: Find it first), which fires electric impulses down the pudendal nerve to the spine, which then builds an orgasmic platform (much faster than your average builder and with no tea breaks). This results in all sorts of reflex muscular activity which is impossible to control.

The A-frame kicks off in the vaginal G spot (if you have one), and goes via the pelvic nerve. Not only do you get the orgasmic platform and uncontrollable muscles with this one, but the womb joins in too. If you're really lucky, you get both at roughly the same time (aka the blended orgasm), which I should imagine takes a bit of recovering from.

These terms are a bit technical and only occasionally used during performance. For example:

'Blend me now, you filthy beast.'

Or,

'Just putting up the A-frame, dear.'

'Do you need it for tenting?'

'How many times do I have to tell you? The tent goes up over there.'

What's most interesting about orgasms is that men and women often get most intensity from doing it themselves, which rather gives the game away that if you want better sex, you need to talk to each other.

Where do I find the use-by date on a penis?

A British-made penis should last a lifetime, but it's worth inspecting it carefully before using it. Sores, blisters, warts, tender testicles, an angry red opening and a discharge that appears with the gentlest of shaft squeezes (and not much pleasure) are all signs that a visit to the clinic should trump penetration. Women are less likely to have visible signs of any infection, so it's worth booking a double MOT. Sexual health clinics make an ideal first date. The prescriptions are always free, and they'll throw in some condoms too. And your mother/teacher/GP will never know (unless they happen to be in the clinic at the same time).

Why vinegar strokes?

Not sure. Vinegar strokes signal the pre-orgasmal point of no return for men during the sexual act, and they're accompanied by varied, bizarre, but actually quite touching, facial expressions; the kind you might make if someone gave you a glass of cold cola to quaff on a hot day and it turned out to be malt vinegar. Or maybe you make that face with Coke. Coke strokes. That has a better ring to it. Anyway, it's only a guess.

What's 'gichigich?'

It's a sexual practice enjoyed by the Yap women of the Caroline Islands of the Western Pacific. The woman sits astride the man while he slowly massages her labia with his penis until she reaches orgasm (often more than once, apparently). According to the *Complete Dictionary of Sexology*, 'because of the strenuous nature of this form of coitus, it is usually only practised by young couples before marriage.' Check with your osteopath first.

Do all women shout 'Geronimo' at orgasm?

Nope. Not heard that one at all. Not even close. Might be helpful if they did, as a lot of men fret about not knowing how much pleasure they've given. It's much easier to tell if a man's come. There's usually some end product for you to tactfully avoid swallowing or lying in, or something in the teat of the condom . . . hopefully. Also men tend to nod off fairly soon afterwards, unless you're having an affair in which case those trousers will be back on before you can say: 'Is it in yet?'

For women, it's often easier (and kinder) to fake it, especially if things have been dragging on a while, there's something good on the telly or you've got to an exciting part in your book. If your partner's particularly good at faking it, she probably wants you to live with the delusion that you're a love god, so why would you want to know otherwise? Besides, fake orgasms take as much (if not more) effort than a real one. Even bad sex can be a good aerobic work-out.

Some men claim to be able to affirm orgasm status by their partner's muscle contractions, blotchy rash or change of pulse, but that all sounds a bit clinical to me. If you look into your partner's eyes, they should reveal the emotions of the moment. And whether she's got jaundice.

Another advantage of looking at your partner during sex is that you're less likely to drift. Marriages, and even lives, have ended because the wrong name has slipped out, and there are very few that allow you to make a smart recovery. 'Phil . . . Phil . . . Fill me up,' is one. Roger and Dick are others. Justin is likely to start a fight, whichever way you play it.

What's the correct response to a fanny fart?

'Bless you.' If it happens again, either ignore it, deny it ('I didn't hear anything. Did you hear anything?'), change position or try 'Gesundheit.' 'Who's that strange man farting under the bed?' might be worth a punt, particularly if it turns out to be the case. 'Owzat!' tends to get a mixed reception. Fanny farts occur when air gets trapped in the vagina (often via a hearty rear-entry pump action) and it makes a sensational escape. If symptoms persist, you can either stop and laugh it out, or try what communication experts call 'mirroring'. Try to match them blow for blow with regular farts. Failing that, a succession of loud and very wet raspberries should cover it.

Is bacchanalia anything to do with Burt Bacharach?

No. They don't even have a common root. Bacchanalia is a euphemism for Roman orgies that kicked off around 200 BC in honour of Bacchus (aka Dionysus) the impish god of wine and revelry. Burt has been around a while, enjoyed a few wives and inspired a lot of cheesy foreplay and revelry with his music. Bacchanalia was brutally suppressed by the Roman government in 185 BC. The only song of Burt's that should have been nipped in the bud was 'Wives and Lovers', the 1963 Jack Jones hit, and only then because of Hal David's lyrics:

> *Hey, little girl, comb your hair, fix your make-up*
> *Soon he will open the door.*
> *Don't think because there's a ring on your finger*
> *You needn't try anymore,*
> *For wives should always be lovers, too,*
> *Run to his arms the moment he comes home to you,*
> *I'm warning you . . .*
>
> *Day after day, there are girls at the office,*
> *And men will always be men,*
> *Don't send him off with your hair still in curlers*
> *You may not see him again . . .*
>
> *Blah, blah, blah . . .*

Can cosmic energy give me better orgasms?

Orgasms are largely in the mind, and if you believe cosmic energy might help you hit the spot, then I suppose it could. I'm not aware of any studies comparing cosmic energy with the standard treatment of time, tenderness and a tickly finger. And if you're thinking of marketing a cosmic energy orgasm box, it's already been done. The Austrian-American Wilhelm Reich was a well-regarded psychoanalyst and supporter of women's rights until he went off piste with his 'orgone box' – a telephone booth with random bits of electronic paraphernalia, designed to capture and concentrate primordial cosmic energy and focus it on the genitalia (and elsewhere).

If you sat inside an 'orgone energy accumulator', it could apparently cure you of common colds, cancer and impotence, as well as improving your orgasms. The orgone box sadly didn't work for Dr Reich, who died of a heart attack in November 1957, in Lewisburg Federal Penitentiary, while serving a two-year term for distributing his unproven invention in violation of the Food and Drug Act.

Where can I get me some Yab-Yum?

From your partner, although you'll both have to work for it. Yab-Yum is a Tibetan term for the mystical oneness and wholeness achieved by sexual intercourse, where the male and female combine in an ideal cosmic oneness that resolves all dualities. For many couples, Yab-Yum is more mystifying than mystical. Especially if your partner has just rolled over, farted and fallen asleep.

Should I hand wash my merkin?

Yes. Pubic wigs are not just for those who over-shave or wax, and then feel the chill, but also for dancers and actresses who want to take their underwear off and still comply with certain nudity laws. A merkin can also be used to surprise a male partner by a sudden change of hair colour, and perhaps make him focus a bit more on the vulva (until it attaches to his chin like a goatee limpet and he freaks out).

The merkin was originally devised in 1796 to recover those who'd lost their hair after smallpox, scarlet fever and, later, mercury treatment for syphilis. Others shaved all their body hair off to give the lice less to cling to. When Jenner discovered the smallpox vaccine, the merkin remained popular amongst prostitutes to give clients a choice of bare or hair, and in a range of colours. It's not unheard of to find a confused louse or crab in a merkin, so cleaning is important. However, a merkin is a delicate beast and can easily disintegrate in a hot wash or mate with your partner's football shorts. So tepid hand-sponging is advised.

Whose idea was the missionary position?

The missionary position has been around long before missionaries, but was strongly advocated during Christian excursions into the South Pacific and Africa from the eighteenth century onwards. This was a bummer for the indigenous populations, who had long ago figured out more adventurous and satisfying sexual practices. The missionaries could have learned a trick or two, had they not been beholden to the theory that man was created first, so he had to go on top to show his primacy over woman in all things.

The position only remains popular today because it's the easiest to do in the dark on a lumpy mattress, and it's rare to fall off. A woman usually won't climax during the standard two-minute missionary, but neither does she have to bare her arse in the mirror. It can be spruced up with the Legs Up, the Plough, The Grip and The High Rider (see *Wikipedia* for pictures). These at least give a woman more to do, other than admiring her nails.

As with all positions, success depends largely on how you approach it. Couples who still love each other can do plenty of caressing, touching, affirming, gazing into each others eyes and breathing in unison. Those who are just going through the motions can easily avoid all clitoral, emotional or eye contact. *A Feminist Dictionary* doesn't rate it very highly: 'The missionary position is unknown and unmissed in many cultures.'

What's the best sexual position for losing weight?

Why not try the wheelbarrow? If you just want the exercise, you can take it in turns to be the barrow or the boy, if you want to have sex as well, it's probably best for a man to do the pushing.* You need to be reasonably strong and fit to work up a proper head of steam but it encapsulates all the best bits of making love (teamwork, sudden releases of air and borderline hysteria). If you're really good, you can have sex and walk around at the same time. Just don't go past your Mum's house.

Is it possible to come without looking like a wounded orc?

No, unless you're faking it for the big screen. In Hollywood, beautiful couples (or their body doubles) pretend to climax in magnificent unison with a dazzling white smile and a short-lived squeal. In reality, most men make the orc face in under fifty strokes and many women don't come at all. On the big screen, nobody goes down like a thirsty Labrador or puts a condom on the wrong way round. Brad Pitt doesn't get cramp or keep missing his entrance. And he never slips out and stubs his knob as he gets up to speed. Real sex is ridiculous, stop-start and clumsy. All that matters is that you all enjoy it.

* The reverse wheelbarrow is too hard even for the Kama Sutra.

Should you brush you teeth before oral sex?

After is probably a better idea. Very few genitals notice garlic breath, although I can see the point of protecting your own taste buds with a minty-mouth. The theory goes that brushing before can open up cracks in the gum, making it more likely that infection can pass through but I haven't seen any proof of this. It's safest to suck/blow/spit/slobber/lick through a condom, either whole (on a penis) or cut into a latex square (over a vulva), in which case a dollop of toothpaste helps takes the taste away of the rubberised strawberry. And the frothy mix of saliva and Colgate you can trick a bloke into thinking he's already come.

> *'Look. There's the proof.'*
> *'But how did it get through the condom?'*
> *'Magic.'*
> *'But why does it smell of peppermint?'*
> *'Never mind that. Your turn!'*

My granny used to say: 'Long and thin goes too far in, short and thick does the trick.' Was she right?

Wow. What a granny. And she's right. The most excitable part of the vagina is the outer third, and the vulva is more sensitive still, so there is no reason for humans to have evolved penises more than three inches long (and indeed, many of us haven't). Many sex toys have a little side shoot, like a mutant carrot, which is far more likely to hit the G spot than something the size of a baby's arm holding an apple.

My granny used to say: 'With a tongue like a cow, you can make them go wow.' Was she right again?

Yes.

What's Peggy Lee syndrome?

It's the feeling of disappointment experienced by many young women upon losing their virginity; so named because of Ms Lee's hit song, 'Is that all there is?' If only we'd listened to the B side – 'Foreplay, foreplay, foreplay', featuring a fifteen-minute tongue solo.

SEXUAL DILEMMAS
What should you do if someone dies on you during sex?

First you need to spot that they're unconscious (rather than asleep or in post-orgasmic shell shock) because you may be able to bring them back from the brink. Death during sex is rare, but it usually happens to men, particularly when they're very excited and not terribly fit (e.g. the unfortunate 'motel mid-life crisis reverse cowgirl with a stranger' episode). It's generally a cardiac arrest that causes death, unless you've been playing asphyxiation games, choked on an aphrodisiac or you're allergic to nuts.

Spotting imminent death is not easy because a man's orgasm face may be very similar to his cardiac arrest face. Also, you may have to stop focusing on your own pleasure and open your eyes to figure out what's happening. Often you have a heart attack before your heart stops, so take all chest pain seriously, stop what you're doing, phone 999 and take an aspirin (it halves the size of the dead heart muscle). Not everyone gets chest pain, but any man who complains of not feeling well during sex is likely to be seriously ill.

If you're not sure if a man's unconscious or asleep, squeeze his balls. Hard. If you get no response at all, assume his heart has stopped. If he's on top of you, roll him back and forth until he slides off (not always easy, but more likely to succeed than a turtle flip.) Phone 999 and say you think your partner has had a cardiac arrest. Open the door for the paramedics. Call for help if you can, and try to get him on his back onto the floor (Note: you should have let go of his balls by now).

Assuming he's bare-chested, kneel beside him and start chest compressions. Put one hand over the other, interlock your fingers and press down hard in the centre of his chest at the level of the armpits. You need to push in further than you think to get the heart pumping again (around 4 cm should do it, and don't worry if you hear the odd bone crack). If you do this to the tune of 'Nelly the Elephant' or 'The Archers' theme, you'll be at roughly the right speed (around 100 compressions a minute). 'Stayin' Alive' works too. 'Another one bites the Dust' is not so funny if it's read out in court.

When you've done thirty good chest compressions, you can do two mouth-to-mouth breaths. Tilt his chin forward and his head back, pinch his nose, open his mouth, take a deep breath, make a good seal with your lips and blow in hard for a second. Do it twice and then do another thirty compressions, repeating this cycle until the crew arrive (hopefully in eight minutes or less, by which time you'll be absolutely pooped). Don't waste time ferreting around in his mouth for bits of denture/peanut etc. If there's vomit around and you just can't face mouth-to-mouth, continue the compressions until help arrives.

If there's just one of you, you may find it easier to do chest compressions kneeling at the head end. Quickly slip some pants on, or it may look awkward when the paramedics arrive. On the other hand, if he comes round it's a win-win.

Resuscitation rarely happens when people collapse, even if it's got nothing to do with sex, because so few of us can be bothered to learn how to do it properly. There are loads of courses out there, but even when we've learnt, you can never be sure how you'll react when shit happens. Time is of the essence. So to recap: Man on top not moving? Squeeze balls hard. If he wakes up, apologise. If no response, roll him off and phone 999. Put your pants on if you can (but don't waste time with his). Call for help (may not be practical). Repeat cycle of thirty chest compressions and two breaths until help arrives. If the mouth is full of unmentionables, just keep doing the chest compressions.

If your partner has a stroke, his or her speech may become incomprehensible and the face strangely asymmetrical (again not always easy to spot during sex). Sudden weakness down one side the body is definitely abnormal. Phone 999. Fast.

NOTE: The French have a phrase called 'mort douce', (sweet death). It can mean death during sexual intercourse, the warmth and calm that follows a (living) orgasm or voluntary euthanasia. Worth knowing if you're calling for help abroad.

Can a corpse have an erection?

See above. Even if sex doesn't kill you, you can still appear to have a hard-on if you die face down, due to the gravitational pooling of the blood, muscle stiffening from lactic acid build up (rigor mortis) and bloating from bacterial gas release. The result is pretty impressive, known in America as 'angel lust' and down my local undertaker's as 'Satan's club'. The observation in the seventeenth century that a hanged man could get angel lust led to a (mercifully brief) fad of deliberate asphyxiation as a cure for erectile dysfunction. Other treatments are available.

Should the NHS pay for erections?

I think so, but not everyone agrees. Sex is important to many (but certainly not all) couples and treating erectile dysfunction can save relationships and keep families together. But the British have hang-ups about sex and pleasure, so treatment is ridiculously rationed and only given to those with listed diseases. As one tight-arsed manager told me:

> *I don't think the NHS should pay for Viagra. I mean, sex is fun but you can do without it. It's not something you have to do, like cutting the lawn, which I find distinctly unpleasurable. In fact, if the state is going to pay for men to have sex, they ought to pay for someone to cut my lawn. That'd give me far more pleasure than a handful of blue pills.*

My pro-treatment view was shaped by a wonderful nurse specialist called Sister Nolly: 'A penis is not for stirring the tea. I give men erections.' And with a strike rate of over ninety per cent, few people could argue with her claim to be 'a tool hardener'. Nolly's clinic is unusual in that she runs it without a clumsy doctor sticking his beak in. She's got a very understanding reception team and an angle-poise mirror to help plump men locate their penises. After that, it's all down to Nolly.

'For the first consultation, I don't lay a finger on them. I just listen.' Nolly has amazing stories of men who haven't managed an erection for twenty years of married life but have never had the guts to seek help, or even known that help was available. Often, there's a great outpouring of missed opportunity. Nolly encourages partners to attend, and frequently the women are as guilt-ridden as the men. 'The men blame the women, the women blame

themselves, and the whole marriage falls to pieces.' However, the effect of treatment can be equally profound. Couples go in with hunched shoulders and leave walking on sunshine. I don't know many NHS treatments that manage that.

What is the minimal acceptable firmness for an erection?

Sex therapists talk in terms of marshmallow, tofu, banana and cucumber. I suspect tofu is for the middle-class clients, but the bottom line is if it works, it's firm enough. If you're not sure, keep an emergency courgette under the mattress.

Can a postage stamp spot an erection?

The stamp test is used to separate those men who have trouble getting hard most of the time (usually a physical cause), and those who get very anxious during the day but swell up in their sleep. You put a strip of stamps snugly around the penis on retiring and if you go hard, the perforations break. And you can still use the stamps afterwards, with an amusing PS. 'Here's one for your collection' or 'You'll never guess where these have been!'

Does the size of an erection pill matter?

Only if you can't swallow it. There are three different tablets you can take for erectile dysfunction (more on the way) Sildenafil, trade name Viagra, is a blue diamond. Then there's Vardenafil (Levitra, orange circle) and Tadalafil (Cialis, mustard yellow egg). There have been no 'head-to-head' comparisons between the three so it's hard to say which is best and it's down to which works best for you. Overall, they work in about seventy per cent of men, seventy per cent of the time. None of them are aphrodisiacs — you have to be in the mood to kick things off.

Cialis hangs round in the blood stream for longer, which may mean you can have sex more than once in thirty-six hours (perish the thought). Levitra claims to have a slightly better strike rate the first time you use it. Viagra needs to be taken an hour before sex and the effect can be delayed by food. Levitra is swallowed at least twenty-five minutes before the off but can be delayed with a high-fat meal. Cialis doesn't seem to be effected by food and you can take it thirty minutes before sex, but you might find another erection pops up twenty-four hours later, which may not always be convenient.

Viagra is the iconic brand leader and some men find just having the little blue diamond on the bedside locker is enough to give them a psychological fillip. However, it is very recognisable and if you'd rather be more discreet about your pharmacological enhancement, you might be better choosing an alternative that looks like a multivitamin.

You can't take these tablets if you're on other drugs called nitrates and get advice if you've recently had a heart attack or a stroke. All men get erectile dysfunction occasionally (e.g. when you're asked to do it again before you've had a kip) but if it persists, your penis may be telling you something important, like you're clinically depressed, drinking too much or your arteries are furring up. If you're worried about the reception you'll get, tell the receptionist it's about your cholesterol.

Does anyone inject his penis anymore?

Yes. Men with erectile dysfunction who can't take, or don't respond, to tablets can inject a drug called Alprostadil into the side of the penis. This requires a steady hand and can take a bit of getting used to, so it's generally best if a doctor or nurse shows you how to do it before you have a go. You need to dissolve the drug in water, draw it up via needle and syringe, keep the skin over the side of the penis taught and go in at right angles, near the base and on the side, avoiding any visible veins. After the needle comes out, you compress with an alcohol swab for a minute and presto. One erection.

The most troublesome side-effect is priapism – an erection that won't go away. It happens in one in a hundred men and makes a great party trick to begin with. If it's still there after four hours, or your guests are getting bored, you should think about getting help. After six to eight hours on the hard, your penis clots off and is irreversibly damaged, so well before that, you need to make one of those ever-so-slightly embarrassing trips to casualty, where we draw out the blood through a small needle whilst chatting cheerily about the weather.

Can you choose what size penis you'd like with vacuum pump?

Within limits, yes. Just about any man can get an erection with a vacuum pump. The design was patented in 1917 by Dr Otto Lederer and hasn't changed much since. You put a plastic tube, with a bit of lube on the seal side, over your penis and pump air out of the other end (or use a battery-operated version to do it for you). When the vacuum pressure reaches around 100mm of mercury, blood is drawn into the penis. You, or your partner, can choose between small, medium or large, but you mustn't push your luck and over-pump, or you risk swelling and bruising.

The erection is maintained by sliding a cock ring down the tube and over the base. It's good to go for thirty minutes maximum, before it becomes a bit painful and if you leave it on too long, it can clot off. Not pretty. The erection itself can be mightily impressive but it's stone-cold and bluish, and the cock ring can stem the flow of semen and make things a bit wobbly at the base. But plenty of couples manage just fine with it and, if money's a bit tight, you can share the pump with your neighbours.

TIP: Get to know them first.

ANOTHER TOP TIP: If you're happy with the size of your erection but have trouble maintaining it, a cock ring alone could help. Choose one that isn't too tight and with a handle or two on the side, so you can get it off again, or you'll be dashing up to casualty.

Is it safe to fall asleep with a penis enlarger on?

No. But it's generally a mistake you only make once. It was on my paper round that I first came across Dr Chartham and his revolutionary penis enlarger. One of the customers down Elcot Lane used to have a *Fiesta* delivered with his *Times*, once a month. It would come in on a Friday but I wouldn't deliver it until the Monday (at least I didn't until I was caught taking it home).

As well as acquainting myself with views of the female anatomy not found in my biology textbook, I spotted an ad that promised to put three inches on length and an inch on girth. I already had ginger hair, glasses and freckles. What I needed was a unique selling point. So I donated my savings to the good Dr C, who had the decency to send me his device in plain packaging. I told Mum it was a gemstone polisher (I was a keen rock collector at the time).

The enlarger was just a cheap vacuum pump; rubber seal at one end and a hand pump at the other. It turned a frankfurter into a king salami until you took it off again, when it shrank back to its original size. Dr Chartham evidently realised this, and only guaranteed improvements if you persevered with his regime every night for twelve weeks. This included an exercise routine which involved wrapping your penis in a warm flannel to improve the blood supply, followed by half an hour's passive stretching. Being quite hormonal at the time, I seldom got past five minutes.

It required a lot of commitment and privacy, which I could only guarantee after lights out. My school work started to suffer. Four weeks into the programme, I fell asleep with the enlarger on. Dr Chartham warned against breaching the thirty minute limit; I had it on for eight hours.

I woke to find my penis reincarnated as a cylindrical blancmange, eight inches long, three inches wide and completely useless. It flopped around like a broken windscreen wiper. I felt no pain until I tried to locate my foreskin, which was grossly swollen, constricting the blood supply to the end and refusing to unravel. I had visions of having to go cock-in-hand to the casualty department, before a superhuman tug restored some semblance of anatomy. But would it ever be hard again (other than just hard to explain)?

Medicine has apparently advanced since then, and it's now possible to have corrective surgery to answer (or rather exploit) man's greatest insecurity. Those who present themselves to private penis enlargement clinics tend to be in their thirties or forties and from all walks of life. The vast majority have penises that are well within the anatomical norms, but then cosmetic surgery has always relied more on perception than truth. What they all have in common is a few thousand quid's worth of disposable income. That's an awful lot of paper rounds.

There are, broadly speaking, two types of operation; wideners and lengtheners. Adding width is less risky and relies on 'reverse liposuction', in which four ounces of fat is taken from the abdomen and injected beneath the penile skin. In theory, more fat could be injected because the skin of the shaft is very stretchy, but as yet there is no way of swelling the head and it pays to keep a sense of proportion; a cherry atop a cucumber looks faintly ludicrous. The transplanted fat cells also have a tendency to clump up, giving the penis a rather bumpy profile. After vigorous sex, you can also get a snowdrift effect. The fat migrates to the base of your penis, which then ends up looking like a parsnip.

The extra girth can also result in a loss of sensation, akin to wearing a lard condom, and if you're really unlucky you can end up with a soft tissue infection known as 'cellulitic dick'. Sex is prohibited for one month after the operation, to stop permanent fat drift. However, in most cases it is possible to suck any miscreant fat back out again.

Adding length requires an unshakeable belief in the omnipotence of your surgeon. It entails cutting the group of ligaments that anchor the base of the penis to the underside of the pelvic bone and pulling out the root of your penis that normally lies anchored above your scrotum. This gives you an extra inch or so on show at the risk of going a bit wobbly at the base. Another windscreen-wiper dick. Also, your penis may not stand up so high as it used to and if a nerve gets cut, it may not stand up at all. In addition, the tug forward often means that pubic hair will sprout half way up your shaft. Some men are curiously dissatisfied with their sex life after surgery: 'Look, I've given you a huge-numb-hairy-parsnip-wiper. What more do you want?'

Some women like a big dick, most prefer a clean one, a kind heart and a sense of adventure. The most erogenous zones are near the surface of the body and deep in the mind.

Is it normal to squirt during sex?

If you're a bloke, yes, although it's good manners to ask permission first. Some women also release a stream of fluid either on penetration or at orgasm. As far back as 1950, German gynaecologist Ernst Grafenberg (he of G-spot fame), claimed this was the female equivalent of ejaculation, and was most likely to happen if his (or rather her) G spot was stimulated. This spot is located on the anterior wall of the vagina, only an inch or two in, so even the modestly endowed have a chance of happening upon it, halfway between the back of the pubic bone and the front of the cervix (which is no use at all if you don't know your anatomy). Alternatively, gently stroke the front wall of the vagina and see if you can find an area of intense sensitivity. Not everyone seems to have one, but it's lots of fun searching.

In the seventeenth century, a Dutch embryologist called Regnier de Graaf described small glands surrounding the urethral opening in women which produced a fluid 'which makes women more libidinous with its pungency and saltiness'. 200 years later, these were formally named Skene's glands, after the Scottish gynaecologist Alexander Johnston Chalmers Skene. These are the equivalent of the male prostate, and both produce an enzyme called acid phosphatase. The prostate also produces lots of clear fluid to give sperm some zip on the way out. But do Skene's glands produce a womanly ejaculate?

In the 1930s, Dutch gynaecologist Theodore H. Van de Velde observed:

> *It appears that the majority of laymen believe that something is forcibly squirted or expelled from the woman's body in orgasm, and should so happen normally, as in the man's case . . . I cannot venture to decide whether it should so happen, according to natural law. There is no doubt that it does happen to some women. But whether these are a majority or minority I am unable to determine.*

We could just have left it there and enjoyed the spectacle, but science is relentless in seeking out answers to academic questions. Such as 'is the spurty stuff lady cum or wee?' Certainly women who've braved childbirth a few times find that they can leak a bit during hop-skip-cough-giggle-sex games. But studies to find out what precisely is released on orgasm have been scant and poorly attended. In one group of six women, the acid phosphatase levels of what was quickly scooped up were similar to urine. But a tiny study of just one woman found she had levels equivalent to prostatic fluid.

Who cares? If you enjoy the visual treat of a golden stream or even a clear one, and have a ready supply of old towels, then let it be. If you don't, have a pee before sex and see if it makes a difference. If wee is an unwelcome guest on other occasions, see your GP. There's plenty that can be done. Just tell the receptionist you've come about your prostate.

Is it possible to have a dry orgasm?

For a woman, almost certainly not. Dryness usually indicates a negligent amount of foreplay, a lack of desire or a lack of oestrogen, and sex is likely to be painful and unfulfilling. If Tony Blair's mantra had been 'Foreplay, foreplay, foreplay' he'd have left a far greater legacy. Blokes can have 'dry taps', when they're young and masturbating all the time, when they're old and the sperm shoots the wrong way into the bladder, when they've had prostate surgery or when they've got a cock ring on so tight that the semen can't get through.

Why do women get cystitis on their honeymoon?

On an ideal honeymoon, you'd get the chance to pee before sex (to prevent leakage) and after sex (to flush out any bowel bugs that have slipped upwards). But when you're having lots of sex, the pee break can get overlooked. The urethral opening (wee hole) is mid-way between the clitoris (above) and vaginal opening (below), and it can get bruised and inflamed during sex, making infection more likely and sex less gratifying. Have a breather. And point out the regular pee breaks in the small print of your marriage contract.

Can you fracture a penis?

Yes. Even though a human penis has no bone, you should never try to bend it in half (no matter how big it is). This most often happens accidentally when a woman – understandably surprised and enthused about going on top for once – comes down hard and you both miss the point of entry. If you're lucky, it just hurts a bit. If you're very unlucky and you've got your hearing aid in, you might hear a crack or pop – followed by extreme pain, immediate flaccidity and impressive bruising.

Forget NHS Direct ('dead dick, dead dick, dead dick, dead dick . . . would you say it's diabetes at all?') and go straight to casualty. In the old days, we used to treat penile fracture with cold compresses and splinting, but now we tend to favour immediate surgical repair. However, this really is the occasion to ask 'Have you done one like this before?'

Can you bite off a penis by accident?

It happens. *Cosmopolitan* often extols the gentle use of the teeth to enhance a man's pleasure. The key word here is 'gentle.' And occasionally, it can be hard to remember what you've got in your mouth, especially if it's been there for ages and you were feeling a bit peckish to start with. As a rule of thumb, a gherkin doesn't have a man attached to it.

But accidents still happen. There's a famous scene in *The World according to Garp* when a couple fellating illicitly in a car are shunted from behind with the lights off. Then there's the famous Shrove Tuesday trauma, when a man pitched up to casualty with a severed penis, accompanied by his girlfriend who had a burn on her face and bruising at the back of the scalp. The man had been cooking romantic pancakes for two, bottle of bubbly open on the side, Classic FM on the digital radio. His partner decided to show her appreciation down below. Distracted man tosses pancake. Distracted man misses pancake. Red-hot pancake flips onto woman's forehead. Shocked woman bites penis. Man taps woman on head with saucepan to get her to let go. Bad idea.

This is one of the few occasions in life when a prior health and safety assessment might have made a difference. The addition of a safety net would have prevented a lot of trauma and salvaged a good pancake. You can contact the Health and Safety Executive on 0845 345 0055. Why not phone now, while the batter's standing?

Should semen be part of a calorie-controlled diet?

I think 'could' is a better ask. Each loving spoonful contains the same number of calories as five cans of Diet Coke, without the burping. The most nutritious stuff probably comes from the prostate, which adds its salty secretions to give the sperm some zip. There's also vitamin C, citric acid, zinc, prostaglandins and all sorts of things you'd pay good money for in a health food shop. Most of it is simply water, though it may taste better out of the tap.

Does that bum love-patch work?

I'm not sure. Pharmaceutical giants Procter and Gamble launched a testosterone patch for women in 2008, which is supposed to 'stimulate thoughts about sex.' Its use is meant to be restricted to those who've had a premature menopause and – having enjoyed a good sex-drive previously – are now short of testosterone and need a bit of hormonal help. However, as with testosterone supplements for men, it's sure to be demanded (or bought over the internet) by people with normal levels of the hormone who are desperate enough to try anything. 'Go on, love, slap it on your bum and bend over.'

And even for women with low testosterone levels, there are plenty of non-hormonal reasons not to want sex. What desperate housewife wouldn't jump at the chance of rekindling a flame long since extinguished by a sullen husband, four hyperactive kids and an abusive boss? Why all you need is a sticky patch on the buttock.

If you've had a premature menopause then a bit of testosterone might be worth a shout. Indeed, some gynaecologists suggest testosterone implants if the ovaries have been removed. But Intrinsa is just the first of twenty 'female sex-drugs' under development. And to have any chance of success, first you have to convince people that they have a problem that needs treating, rather than a natural waning of libido or a desire to pursue other pleasures not involving sex.

Unbelievable as it sounds, there are people out there who don't want sex all the time, but we're jolly lucky to have a diligent drug industry determined to find a multi-billion pound magic potion to cure us all. And let's not forget Dr Gillian McKeith's Fast Formula Horny Goat Weed Complex herbal sex pills.

As for the testosterone patch, my Gran swears by it. She's far more assertive and way out of the front of the pension queue. That's if you can get her out of the bedroom. She's got just one side effect though. She's got a little bit of unwanted hair . . . on her penis. Still, that's medicine for you . . . swings and roundabouts.

NOTE TO PROCTER AND GAMBLE'S LAWYERS. This is just a gag.

I accept that there is no evidence a testosterone patch, properly applied, will make a woman grow a penis. There is, however, evidence to suggest that for women with low testosterone, Intrinsia gives them 'an average of 1.9 additional satisfying sexual episodes a month, compared to 0.5 with a placebo'.

Do men who suffer from premature ejaculation turn up early to their appointments?

Often they do. A feeling of time pressure is at the heart of the matter.

Do you need a stopwatch to diagnose premature ejaculation?

No. Someone on the sidelines shouting 'ready, steady, cock' is only likely to make it worse. Of course it's happened, because doctors are anal about measuring things properly. When you just ask men about their performance, they may deliberately lie or just not be aware of the time. Even so, the famous *Hite Report on Male Sexuality* (1981) found that most of us lift off fairly quickly. Of 11,239 men aged thirteen to ninety-seven, sixty-two per cent said they came within five minutes of penetration, twenty-one per cent didn't last a minute and one lost his dentures. Seven per cent claimed they did not ejaculate before fifteen minutes, but that probably included a ten-minute kip in the middle.

In a recent 'stopwatch multinational study of a random heterosexual population' the most common 'intravaginal ejaculation latency time' (IELT) was 5.4 minutes. Or to paraphrase the O'Jays, when people all over the world join glands and start a love train, it usually doesn't last much longer than the song. The researchers proposed that coming within a minute of penetration was 'definite premature ejaculation'.

But even then, it's not that simple. If you and your partner are happy with just a minute (and who wouldn't be for anal sex?), then you have absolutely nothing to worry about. You'd be surprised how many people want to get it over fairly quickly so they can turn on Radio 4 . . . especially if you're bending over in the bushes on Bushey Heath. You've only got premature ejaculation if you usually come before you want to, you can't delay it by thinking of the day your dog died, and you lie awake bothering about it afterwards, stop enjoying sex or stop sex altogether. And that would be a pity.

How hard should you squeeze to stop the semen geyser?

Hang on. There are a few things to work through before we get onto the squeezing bit. Getting it out in the open is a good start, but many couples don't talk much before, during or in-between sex. They don't look each other in the eye to spot the anguish. If one tries to talk, the other rolls over. So the problem may only fully surface when you split up. As Loudon Wainwright III once put it:

> *We used to be in love*
> *But now we are in hate*
> *You used to say I came too early*
> *But it was you who came to late*

NOTE: Loudon Wainwright (father of Rufus and Martha) is a star, not least for his honesty and humour in articulating a man's lot. I once followed him into a toilet in Edinburgh and said – as we peed together – 'Loudon, you're my hero.' He countered with a firm, 'Steady, boy.' But I got his autograph.

If you always come quickly, and always have done with all partners, and you see a doctor who's on the case, you're likely to be offered a drug called an SSRI. If you have lots of sex, you may decide to take one every day, or just take one six hours before you need it (not always easy to plan). In one study, the drugs helped men hang on nearly nine times longer, but three to four times would seem to be the average. SSRIs can have side effects (fatigue, yawning, mild nausea, loose stools, perspiration, agitation, diminished libido and – ironically – erectile dysfunction). For some men, they're a life changer, others can't stand them.

Alternatively, you can buy a local anaesthetic spray (subtly called Premjact. Just the thing in a busy Boots). This gets sprayed on the head of your penis ten minutes before sex and takes away a bit of sensation. If you cover it with a condom too, you'll lose a little bit more friction and the anaesthetic spray won't rub off on your partner. Alternatively, buy a condom with anaesthetic already in it. Durex Performa is one, although you may end up uncomfortably numb.

If you've only recently started coming quickly with a new partner, or if you don't fancy taking any drugs, then you can have a lot of fun learning to hold on, provided (as with all sex) you keep a sense of humour and perspective.

Things you can do for yourself include a tug before sex (only really works below a certain age), wear a condom (on your penis), make shorter thrusts or circular motions, have a break, take it out quickly and squeeze the head, go fishing for the condom, remember to hold onto the base of the condom when withdrawing next time, put on a new condom, pop it back in, name the 1966 World Cup winning team (preferably not out loud), laugh, take a deep breath and clench your buttocks repeatedly near climax. Then go again as soon as you're both up to it.

The anus-tightening exercise is good for men (to hold on longer) and women (to keep their pelvic floor intact). If you're competitive, you can have a clench-off in the queue at Asda (**TIP**. Make sure you've mastered the neutral clench-face first). A hundred clenches a minute is a fantastic score (and the same rate you pump a heart after a cardiac arrest).

Other things you can do together include talking, listening, laughing, looking at each other, foreplay, more foreplay for her and afterplay if required. The squeeze technique is much more fun together, provided it isn't done too hard. Just as some men try to find the G spot by turning their hand into a human egg-whisk and hoping for the best, many women 'stroke' a man as if they were de-rooting a tree in double-time. Handle each others parts with care. Start slow and gentle, and use eye contact and affirmation to change the pace.

> *The squeeze technique: Chat, kiss, cuddle, hand-stoke the penis, feel the pleasure but give the stop sign before you come. Gesturing with a down-turned palm is a good sign, or shouting 'Nobby Stiles.' Quickly but gently squeeze just below the head of the penis for twenty seconds. Chat, laugh, do fifty anal clenches, remember Jimmy Greaves and relax for thirty seconds. Start again. Repeat three times and then come. If you come sooner, who cares? Next time, try it with some lubricant. When you've built up a bit of stamina, have sex with your partner on top (or underneath, if you'd prefer) and use the same stop-start signals.*

The good news is that nearly all couples find this method helps, the bad news is that it takes a lot of patience and you may need to persevere several times a week for several months. Not really something for a one-night stand. In the longer term, the mere fact that you're concentrating on each other's pleasure and looking at each other will do more for your sex life than just a minute staring at a pillow.

MAKING BABIES
Why does it take a hundred million sperm to fertilise on egg?

Because none of them will stop to ask the way.

Are you more likely to make a baby with one big shot or lots of little shots?

It might seem logical to save all your sperm up for one huge explosion in the middle of the cycle, but fertilisation is more likely to occur the more often you have sex. Although you release fewer sperm each time, they move faster and have more chance of bumping into an egg. Your position or the phase of the moon makes no difference to the odds of fertilisation but it never hurts to lie down and cuddle for a while afterwards.

Is it true that a horny fish can tell you if you're pregnant?

Nearly. An old folk pregnancy test was to catch a female bitterling (looks a bit like a carp, apparently) and you pop it in a quart of fresh water with two teaspoons of urine from the woman being tested. If she's pregnant, the fish will stick out its impressive ovipositor (egg-laying tube), or so the theory goes. The non-excited ovipositor is only 2mm long, but bigs up to 25 mm, so it's easier than a standard pregnancy test to read.

When this old wives' tail was put to the test in 1936, twenty-eight urine samples of women known to be pregnant were tested, and the bitterling popped out its egg tube for twenty-six within twenty-four hours, and the other two within forty-eight hours. So far so good; a sensitive test. Alas, the tube also popped out for three menstruating women, three men, two children and one post-menopausal woman. We now have much more specific pregnancy tests so we can let the bitterling be.

Don't feel too sorry for bitterlings. The ladyfish have such long ovipostors so they can deposit their eggs between the gill filaments of freshwater mussels. Before the mussel has time to object, the male bitterling ejects his sperm into its water current, fertilisation occurs and the parents then bugger off upstream, leaving the mussel to raise their kids.

How can I tell if my cervix is ripe?

Nearly every pregnant doctor I've known has examined her own cervix. This is more out of curiosity than fear, to assess the ripeness. For those who've never tried, a normal cervix is firm and long, like a carrot. By the end of pregnancy, it goes soft and mushy, like a warm marshmallow. Desperate doctors have even been known to give it a quick 'sweep' to try to bring on labour. At forty-two weeks with heartburn, backache and piles, you'll try anything.

The official test or ripeness is not a squeeze, but something called the Bishop Score. Bishops seem to get everywhere these days, but this one was an obstetrician who wanted to predict if the cervix was ready to get labour started. There are six factors to be scored from nought to three by internal examination but in essence, if yours is a carrot, there's no way the baby's coming out that way anytime soon (no matter how much wheelbarrow sex you have while eating a vindaloo). If, on the other hand, you're getting warm marshmallow, keep your birth plan with you at all times.

Can men appear to be pregnant?

A lot of men have the shape of a pregnant woman, thanks to the Budweiser baby*, but they can also have the symptoms to go with it, described by the French as 'couvade' (from couver, meaning to brood or hatch). Couvade has been documented in most Western cultures with a surprising number of fathers-to-be suffering from nausea, vomiting, heartburn, constipation, backache, headache, restlessness, poor sleep, poor concentration, irritability, fatigue, tension, odd food cravings and even more weight gain than the beer can explain.

Some men even go through quite convincing motions of labour pain and delivery, seen in some cultures as a way of sharing the burden and drawing evil spirits away from the mother, and something to be praised and celebrated. In the West, you're likely to be labelled as neurotic and told to pull yourself together or get out of the room. There are, however, weighted corsets you can buy or borrow to experience the equivalent mechanical challenge of lugging a baby around inside you. But they do look silly.

Can I demand a Caesarean section to keep my fanny honeymoon-fresh?

You can certainly ask for it, but you may have to convince your obstetrician that a honeymoon-fresh fanny is 'an established clinical need'. In your favour is the fact that a fair few doctors and doctors' wives take the Caesarean route to save their pelvic floor from the ravages of a ten-pounder with a prop's shoulders. But a Caesarean section has its own risks, and costs a lot more than pushing-as-directed.

As a doctor, I was only ever called to deliveries that went

*Other beers are available

wrong and so my perception of childbirth (a painful mess where babies invariably get stuck and vaginas are torn to shreds before being sewn up the wrong way round) is at odds with the normal, head-first, joyous, anatomy-preserving birth that most people apparently have.

The last birth I witnessed was one of the most pleasant; a planned Caesarean section under a spinal block. I was filming a documentary about the history of anaesthetics, and how we've gone from theatrical amputations on screaming patients, to knocking everyone out by taking them as close to death as possible and, finally, keeping them awake and completely pain free. The birth was in the latter camp, and very moving. Nobody argues that Caesareans don't work – you've got to be pretty bad if you don't manage to get the baby out – but there are still risks from the anaesthetic, operative mishap, blood clots, infections, scar pain and a longer recovery time.

Most women weigh up the evidence and go for route one, but if I was ever pregnant, I'd certainly consider other options. One in ten women have difficulty controlling wind or faeces after childbirth, particularly older mums with big babies. Even more have leakage of urine and it's not uncommon to have both. Because we don't like talking about it, many women have no idea what they're letting themselves in for. Treatments can help, but you may choose not go there in the first place.

Are men damaged by birth?

That's just the start of it. I once went to the pub with a group of new dads, and we shared our experiences and anxieties:

> *'It's great being a Dad. You spend all day worrying about meningitis and all night worrying about cot death. And then you rush out and buy a second-*

hand Volvo Estate and a boot full of smoke alarms.'

'He was really difficult for the first three months – inconsolable and angry – and it rubbed off on us. I was sure his first words would be "little fucker".'

'I don't know why, but I was expecting her to come out beautiful, not all squashed up and covered in blood. She looked like a peeled plum tomato'

'Yeah, but don't they smell lovely.'

'Not at both ends.'

'I never thought I'd see my wife thrashing about, swearing her head off and biting me. Well, not all at once. I don't see why it has to be so painful.'

'I heard it's like shitting a watermelon'

'I heard it's like putting a deflated basketball up your arse, then pumping it up for nine months and then shitting it out.'

'I heard it was like taking your top lip and stretching it back right over your head.'

'I don't think I'll ever recover from the sight of the wife's piles. Bloody enormous. Like the Hanging Gardens of Babylon.'

'My wife had loads of stitches but they wouldn't dissolve so I had to cut them out for her. It looked a right mess down there, and I'm sure she's a flap short. I don't see how sex can ever be the same.'

'Does it feel the same after a baby's passed through?'

'Dunno. Who's had sex yet?'

'No'

'No'

'No'

'Hand job'

'Now we've had a baby, it's no more blow jobs. I don't really understand the logic. I mean, it's not as if they come out of your mouth.'

'Has anyone else got a hole on the underside of his penis?'

(Pause)

'My round, I think'

'No, I'll get it.'

Round 2

'Sorry, you were saying?'

'Nothing.'

'Has anyone changed a nappy yet?'

'No'

'No'

'No'

'No'

'Yes. And it changed everything. For the first three months, I hated being a dad. He suffered from colic and all I could do was stick him in a sling and me in an iPod and pace around the garden for hours. I didn't hate him, I didn't love him. I just wanted to go to bed. Then one day I changed his nappy. I wasn't sure what I was doing and it took ages and he got fidgety. He stuck his hand in his poo, stuck it in my mouth and the bastard smiled at me.

We bonded for life. From then on in, he was pulling my glasses off, copying my raspberries and smiling like a village idiot. In the "who gets on best with the baby?" competition, mothers usually edge it until speech kicks in. Babies find it easier to say "Dada" than "Muma". But you've got to be there to witness it.'

'Have you finished?'

'No. It's hypospadius.'

'What is?'

'The hole in the underside of your knob. It's quite common and I know a brilliant plastic surgeon who can fix it.'

'Oh right. Would you like to see it?'

'Not just now. I'll have another beer, though .'

Can men breastfeed?

Theoretically yes. We have breasts and certain drugs and illnesses have been known to trigger lactation. Breastfeeding, however, is a big step up for men. I know one orthopaedic surgeon, keen to empathise with his wife's sore nipples, who allowed his baby to latch on, just the see what it felt like. He screamed like a . . . well, like a breastfeeding man.

Is it normal to be turned on watching my partner breastfeed?

Hard to say. The sleep-deprived, sex-deprived, emotionally-overloaded new dad can react in all sorts of ways. If something gives you pleasure without harm, then it's OK. I'd just be a bit wary about sharing it with the men's group. Breastfeeding is a fabulous thing and can provide all the nourishment a baby needs for the first six months. So don't interrupt it with an erection. Just hold fire and think of all the money you're saving on formula feeds.

Breasts are very good at multi-tasking, which is why men find them so confusing. They provide occasional visual and tactile stimulation, as well as being hormonally-active throughout life and constantly on standby each month in case they're called into action for infant feeding (which, unbelievably, is what they're for). And if the breasts are working well, a baby doesn't need any more food at all for six months; no topping up with formula or sugary snacks, less chance of an overweight toddler. And there are other benefits of breastfeeding:

For mums, it:

- **strengthens your bones**;
- **lowers your risk of getting ovarian or breast cancer**;
- **gets your figure back more quickly**;
- **makes the nappies stink less.**

For babies, it:

- **protects against diarrhoea, gastroenteritis, ear and chest infections**;
- **reduces the risk of diabetes and eczema**;
- **makes the nappies stink less.**

Some women find breastfeeding a challenge, particularly first time round, but there's a whole army of qualified lactation consultants out there itching to help. To find one near you, go to www.lcgb. org.

Why is the public sign for breastfeeding a bottle?

Because we're a nation of prudes. If we can't even tolerate a breast sign in a motorway service station, what chance a public feast? Breastfeeding takes a lot of time and effort, and it's nice to get out of the house occasionally. But being forced to feed in a filthy public toilet or a stuffy car, because some ignorant prig takes offence at the merest hint of nipple, is absurd. If as many mothers as possible breastfed exclusively for the first six months, it would do more for the nation's health than anything else I can think of. At present, two per cent do. Breastfeeding in public needs to fill the cultural space that smokers have vacated, and soon . . . before we get even fatter.

NOT MAKING BABIES

In an ideal world, contraception would be fun. We'd all help each other put diaphragms in and condoms on, building it into the performance. Amusing pill reminders would be left on post-it notes around the house. Mirena coils would be fitted in M&S, and men would skip gleefully off to the vasectomy clinic. The fact that none of this happens, and we have very high unwanted pregnancy rates, suggest most people view contraception as a pain in the arse (not a method I'd recommend more than once).

Can family planning save the world?

It could certainly help. A friend of mine recently heard Jonathon Porritt speak in Cheltenham. It was an intelligent talk about the perils our planet faces to a cultured audience, with a few minutes for questions. The final one came from a posh woman at the back: 'I appreciate you're trying to be as constructive as possible, but are we fucked?'

'Tough question', said Porritt, 'but regrettably yes, I think we are fucked.' If you want to know why, read the article that even Greenpeace refused to publish at www.jonathonporritt.com. In essence, our problem isn't so much carbon burning, it's that we have too many carbon burners. Western countries may be facing a future manpower crisis but overall, the planet can't sustain the exponential population growth and we don't have a hope in saving the planet without 'responsible fertility management.'

As Porritt puts it:

> *The governments of many of the poorest countries in the world are crying out for financial support for family planning, but are not getting it. The lives of countless millions of women are devastated by their inability to manage their own fertility, and hundreds of thousands die every year because of illegal abortions or complications from unwanted pregnancies. But their voices go largely unheard. On top of all that, every single one of the environmental problems we face today is exacerbated by population growth, and the already massive challenge of achieving an 80% cut in greenhouse gases by 2050 is rendered completely fantastical by the prospective arrival of another 2.5 billion people over the next 40 years.*

Now, I suspect Greenpeace didn't want to publish this because population restriction is a very controversial topic with all sorts of religious sensitivities and charges of coercion. And it also implies that the work of all those charities devoting their lives to getting us to reduce our consumption is pointless if there are just too many consumers out there. There are arguments against, which Porritt neatly demolishes in his article, but the bottom line is simple. Without decent family planning for all, we really are fucked.

My granny used to say: 'Keep it in your trousers.' What did she mean?

I suspect she meant that not having sex is a highly effective method of birth control, and easier to execute if your genitals aren't on display at the time. And learning to say 'no' is nearly as important as learning to hear it.

Can you get pregnant during a period?

Yes. It's rare to get pregnant during a period but not unheard of, especially towards the end. A condom can prevent this and beetroot-stains on the penis, but you may still need an old towel. And remember to take the tampon out first or it may get lodged up high and forgotten about until it starts to pong (and there's a small risk of toxic shock syndrome).

One reason women get pregnant during a period is if they have a short cycle (say twenty-one days) and so the egg pops out on the last day of bleeding. The other is if it's not a period at all. Some women get bleeding in the middle of the cycle, which maybe due to the contraceptive pill but is often due to Chlamydia. Bleeding after sex also needs checking out.

NOTE: Toxic Shock Syndrome (TSS) is mercifully rare, and no one has proved a link with tampons, although they may encourage the growth or entry into the body of a bacteria (staph aureus), which can occasionally produce a life-threatening toxin. A sudden very high temperature (above 38.9°C) vomiting, a skin rash like sunburn, diarrhoea, feeling faint, muscle aches, dizziness and confusion seems a lot to pin on a tampon, which is why TSS is often diagnosed late, but if you get these symptoms (whatever the cause), get help urgently.

More information about TSS is contained in the tampon manufacturer's instruction leaflet, but I've never met anyone who's read it. In summary, the top tampon tips are:

- **wash your hands before and after inserting a tampon**
- **take the wrapper off**
- **always use a tampon with the lowest absorbency you can get away with**
- **alternate tampons with a sanitary towel or panty liner**
- **change tampons regularly, at least as often as directed on the pack**
- **never insert more than one tampon at a time**
- **when using at night, insert a fresh tampon before going to bed and remove it on waking**
- **make sure you remove the last tampon at the end of your period**
- **don't let boys put them in their nostrils; it's not clever and it doesn't prove anything**

How many hands does it take to put a condom on properly?

For someone of average dexterity, three. Condoms can be a bugger to get on properly, unless you do it for a living. A sex worker once showed me how to conceal a condom in your mouth and then secretly pop it onto a banana (not that you'd expect a banana to notice such a thing, but it was for demonstration purposes only).

The point is, if you're expected to put assorted penises in your mouth in the course of a busy night shift, you soon learn how to take the edge off and reduce your risk of infection. She'd also do a quick check on her clients. Anyone with warts, ulcers, blisters, tender balls or a discharge got politely but firmly turned down and given directions to the nearest clinic. The customer is not king if he's got the clap.

Getting a handle on condoms isn't easy. Actually, that might help. They're slippery buggers. By far the most important condom tip is to involve your partner. Think of it as part of foreplay; dressing for the occasion. The rules come with the packet which you won't have with you because the condom's been in your back pocket for a year and through the wash twice.

You need a new, undamaged one. Check the date and the kite mark (no one ever does this), take it out carefully and examine it closely. If you look at it one way, in a good light, the condom comes through the rim on the outside (this the way you want it). Flip it over and it encloses the rim. Try to put it on this way and you'll get really frustrated, wiping a few leaky sperm all over the outside before you realise you've got it the wrong way round. Discard this condom if you've got another.

If your eyesight is going and you can't spot which way round the condom is with the seductive mood lighting, you can either turn the main light on, fetch your condom glasses or get a second opinion from your partner. Preferably all three. Condoms smell funny and even the gooseberry ones taste of old tyres, but anything that helps prevent pregnancy, HIV, hepatitis, herpes, gonorrhoea, syphilis, warts, Chlamydia and premature ejaculation is allowed to smell of old tyres. (**NOTE:** Condoms don't completely prevent any of these. The only way to do that is to cover yourself from head to toe in rubber. Some people enjoy this, but don't forget a breathing hole.)

Before you roll it on, pinch the end to make space for

sperm and remove air bubbles. Don't snag it on sharp nails. Put it on well before any penetration. Don't fall for the old 'let's go bareback for starters' line. The finish line is never as far away as you'd anticipated. If you're going through your full repertoire of two positions, it's worth checking at changeover that the condom is still on. And grab onto the base and withdraw as soon as you've come. Condoms can quickly slip off a wilting penis, and then you've got to fish it out and get emergency contraception. Don't flush condoms because they can block up the plumbing and it's an embarrassing (and expensive) call out.

If you're still young enough to manage sex twice in one session, use a different condom. If you're big enough to burst an average condom, ask for the large ones. If you're too shy to do this (and not many men are), you can buy them easily online. Don't buy condoms with added spermicide; they don't give you extra contraception and they may increase the risk of transmission of HIV and hepatitis.

ANOTHER TOP TIP. It's good to get a condom on in good time, but the penis does have to be erect. Trying to put a condom on a floppy penis is a good aerobic workout (5,000 calories and counting) but ultimately destined to fail. If it just isn't going to happen, that's the time to create a diversion by putting the condom on your head and blowing it up. You may find the release and laughter gets over the performance anxiety and you're good to go again. But please use a new condom.

NOTE: Some people find it amusing to put a condom up one nostril and pull it out of the other. Funny (once) when it works, but I have seen it get stuck and casualty departments are busy enough as it is on a Saturday night (although we could always do with the light relief).

141

Do vegan condoms count as one of your five portions?

Sadly not. German manufacturer Condomi were the first to endorse dairy-free sex, using cocoa powder not casein to make their condoms. They're endorsed by the Vegan Society, have a kite mark and a burst volume of eighteen litres, enough for even the most juiced-up vegan. They come with the usual selection of flavours (I'm told the chocolate is particularly authentic) and there's even a hand-painted zoo tickler.

If you're allergic to latex or want to try something with a different feel, you can buy polyurethane condoms. They're a bit more pricey but you feel the body heat more and you can use them with both water and oil-based lubricants (latex dissolves in oil. *See* **Dr Phil's Man Milk**).

For non-vegans, there are natural membrane (i.e. lambskin) condoms. They're thinner and stronger than latex and apparently permit more sensation. But although they keep the sperm out, they allow some bugs to pass through so they wouldn't be top of my Christmas list.

The first rubber condom with a reservoir for the ejaculate was introduced in 1901 and trade-named Dreadnaught (literally 'fear nothing'). Better, I guess, than 'feel nothing.' If you find a condom in your drawer made of linen or sheep's gut and tied with a ribbon at the bottom, it's likely to be very old indeed and shouldn't be used (although it almost certainly will have been, many times before). However, it might be worth offering it to an auction house, An eighteenth-century condom illustrated with three naughty nuns fetched £3,300 at Christies. If you can knock off a passable Gainsborough on the side of a Mates King Size, your credit crunch worries could be over.

Who was Dr Condom?

The imaginary physician to Charles II who is said to have invented the condom. He didn't . . . because he was imaginary. Although bits of animal gut have been found at Ancient Egyptian excavations that might have been used as condoms, it was the Italian anatomist Fallopio (he of the eponymous tubes) who first described a sheath, made of linen, to protect against syphilis. What the world needs now is a real Dr Condom, spreading the message of proud, responsible and fun condom usage. I'm sure the Green Cross Code man is free. He just needs a few tweaks to the uniform.

Does anyone use female condoms?

I don't and Dr Google doesn't seem to have the sales figures to hand. The Femidom (or in America, Reality) female condom is made of polyurethane, so it's less likely to tear or cause allergic reactions than latex, and any lubrication can be used with it. They're a bit of a fiddle to get in (six inches long, three inches wide, with a ring at each end. The smaller ring at the closed end goes high in the vagina and over the cervix, so at least you learn some anatomy). If both the man and woman are using condoms without telling each other (as can happen in the dark in Epping Forest), they can stick to each other and cause mutual slippage. Then there's the disposal problem. As Jo Brand observed, Epping Forest on a Sunday morning could look like 'a jellyfish graveyard'.

Whatever happened to the Today sponge?

Good question. And whatever happened to Mott the Hoople? The Today sponge is a spermicide-impregnated contraceptive you pop into your vagina and push it up as far as it will go and until it completely covers your cervix. (Note: It's for women only).

You can then have as much sex as you like for twenty-four hours, so long as the sponge stays where it is for six hours after final emission. You have to take it out after thirty hours, because of the (small) risk of toxic shock syndrome. It's not always a doddle to remove (you may have to bear down and break the suction with your finger), but the manufacturers do have a helpline based in America. Failing that, there's always NHS Direct.

The sponge had some production problems a few years back, and your local chemist may not stock it, but I gather it can now be purchased again online. Your chance of getting pregnant with a year of correct sponge use is ten percent, rising to sixteen per cent if you bung it in any old how. These risks are doubled if you've already had kids, because your cervix has opened up a bit and it's harder to cover.

Other barrier methods for women who don't want to use hormones range from old favourites (such as the diaphragm and cervical cap) to new kids on the block (Lea's Shield and FemCap). Overall, they have very few side effects other than the pre-coital fiddling and the fact that they aren't as good at stopping pregnancy as hormonal methods or a copper coil. And only condoms give persistent protection against infection.

Can you do your own vasectomy?

There are all sorts of things you can do with a Swiss army knife, a supple back and a well-angled shaving mirror, but a vasectomy is something I'd leave to an expert. I know a few doctors who've done their own, and the commonest reasons for turning a knife to your own scrotum are 'to see if I can do it', 'to make sure I get enough anaesthetic', and 'so it's done properly.' The last two hardly inspire confidence in the vasectomy industry, but as market forces transform snip clinics into conveyor belts, it's not unheard of for patients to be aware of what's happening down below and for surgeons to remove something other than a piece of vas deferens. One consultant was less concerned about his colleagues' competence than their confidentiality. 'I just didn't want another surgeon to see my penis. Especially one I might come across socially.'

Can you do a vasectomy without a scalpel?

Yes. You could use your teeth (not recommended). Or you could try the no-scalpel method – developed in China in the 1970s, but don't let that put you off. I'd opt for this because the risk of bleeding and pain are reduced. A puncture so small that it may not even need a stitch is made over the vas deferens (the sperm tube, one each side), it's pulled out with tiny forceps and either cut, clipped or cauterised. Some men get quite significant bruising after the snip but I know a bloke who had the no-scalpel method and his wife was so grateful that he had sex the same afternoon (with a condom but after he'd left the clinic).

Generally it takes about twenty ejaculations to clear the back log of sperm in the tubes so, depending how active you are, you need to use contraception for some months afterwards. You're given the all-clear after two consecutive sperm-free samples but here's a tip: See if you can do the samples at home rather than in an NHS side-room overlooking a crowded car park with a much-thumbed copy of *National Geographic* for inspiration.

If you were a teenage girl, what contraceptive method would you choose?

Abstinence sounds inviting. I've seen enough of life on the labour ward to know I wouldn't want to go through childbirth unless it was absolutely necessary. I'm also very bad at remembering to take pills, so I'd probably opt for a small rod of progesterone in my upper arm to stop me having to worry about pregnancy for three years. I'd also insist on condoms every time and I'd inspect every penis meticulously in a good light before letting it near me. And I'd learn to say 'no', in forty-seven languages.

What's a Coca Cola douche?

A very ineffective method of contraception. Known affectionately down our way as 'a poke and a coke', some young women have sex round the back of Leigh Delamere services and then try to wash out the sperm with a jet of their favourite carbonated thirst-quencher. The theory is that both the pressure of the drink and its mild acidity will wash out and kill sperm, but it may just force sperm up higher and through the cervix. And it doesn't matter which brand you choose, because none of them work. To be fair to the Coca-Cola company, it has spent a tiny portion of its monumental profits trying to dissuade girls from the practice. And there are some very effective methods of post-coital contraception that work up to 120 hours after the event and don't leave a big frothy puddle on lino.

Should I keep emergency contraception in the pantry?

Possibly not the pantry, but it's not a bad idea to have a home supply (somewhere memorable, out of reach of dogs and children). Emergency contraception used to be called the morning after pill, but: a) you don't have to wait until the morning after; and b) it still has a reasonable chance of preventing pregnancy up to 120 hours after spillage. It works best the sooner you take it, and by rebranding it 'emergency contraception', it gives you the hint that: a) it's an emergency; and b) you needn't be shy about asking for help. (e.g. 'The doctor's really busy at the moment. Is it an emergency?' 'Yes.')

You can choose between a single dose of a drug called levonorgestrel (marketed as Levonelle 1500) or a copper coil. Levonelle can be kept in-between the bandages and the TCP for use at your discretion. The coil needs to be fitted by someone who knows what they're doing (preferably a health professional). Levonelle is available free on prescription from any GP practice or walk-in centre and, in some parts of the UK, you can get it free from the chemist without a prescription (often restricted to those under twenty years) For everyone else, you can buy it over the counter for £25 (cheaper than a baby, but still ridiculously expensive). If you take it within twenty-four hours, your chance of not getting pregnant is reduced by ninety-five per cent, which is pretty good odds.

The copper coil is even more effective, but finding a fitter isn't always easy on a Bank Holiday weekend. In America, adolescents can be given a prescription for emergency contraception (known as Plan B) at any visit, so they always have one to hand. In the UK, it's left to the doctor's discretion (one of many reasons why we have such high teenage pregnancy rates). But it's not just teenagers who need it. The second most vulnerable group to unplanned pregnancy are middle-aged women, back out there after a divorce, whose dating skills are a little rusty and they forget to buy the condoms with the Sauvignon Blanc. It also puts them at risk of infection. If I had a pound for every time I heard: 'I'm fifty-three, I can't possibly have gonorrhoea ...'

Do all lady doctors have a Mirena coil?

Not all of them, no, but a recent 'hands up' at a contraceptive meeting I went to suggests quite a few of them do. Mirena is 'a hormone releasing intrauterine system', so if you can't remember the trade name you've got next to no chance of finding out about it. Think of a coil that also releases a very low dose of levornogestrel, the same hormone used for emergency contraception. It's been around since 1995, is fitted (by someone who's been properly trained) through the cervix in the first week of a cycle, stays in for five years, and is very, very, very effective at stopping pregnancy. And it's reversible; your fertility returns when it's taken out.

It also reduces blood loss during periods (very helpful if you're a heavy bleeder) and reduces period pain. On the down side, it can occasionally cause breast pain, fluid retention and acne. It also costs around £80 (nine times more than a copper coil), so you may not be offered it unless you ask. But over five years, it works out as very cheap contraception and you save a fortune on sanitary towels.

Can you use cervical mucus to make string curtains?

During ovulation, cervical mucus can indeed be stretched out to impressive length, something known by the curiously Germanic term, Spinnbarkheit, but I'd need photos to be convinced you can make string curtains out of it. The stretchiness of cervical mucus forms the basis of a natural birth control method pioneered by two Australians, Dr John and Evelyn Billings. When the mucus is at its most slippery, like an egg-white stalactite, it facilitates the passage of sperm through the cervical canal and it's a sign that you shouldn't have sex if you want to avoid pregnancy. The Billings Method is perhaps not the most reliable method of birth control (John and Evelyn had nine children, all planned, apparently) but it's cheap, hormone free, the Pope loves it and it does make a great party trick.

NOTE: Several other 'fertility-awareness-based' methods are available. At the very least, they're a good biology lesson but they require far more time, diligence and commitment, and better eyesight, than many couples can muster.

Which is harder? Remembering to take the pill or remembering what to do if you forget to take it?

I'd never remember to take a pill every day, which is why I'd go for something longer acting (and reversible). Some combined pills require a week off, which would confuse me even more, but you can get packs that have dummy pills in so you take a pill every day, with whatever daily ritual you've chosen to associate it with (tooth brushing, eyebrow plucking, cat feeding).

If you forget a pill, you need an amazing memory to remember what to do. So I've written it out in full . . .

If you're on a progesterone only pill, you have to take it at roughly the same time every day, unless you're on Cerazette, which gives you twelve-hours' leeway (but is more expensive so you may have to push for it).

If you've missed just one pill by less than three hours (twelve hours for Cerazette):

- Relax. Take a pill as soon as you remember, and take the next one at the usual time. You're protected from pregnancy.

If you're more than three hours late (or twelve hours on Cerazette):

- Relax. Take a pill as soon as you remember. If you've missed more than one pill, still only take one at a time.
- Take your next pill at the usual time, even if means taking two pills in one day.
- You are not protected against pregnancy for two days. Continue to take your pills as usual, but use an extra method of contraception,

149

such as condoms, for those days. Or don't have sex. If you've already had unprotected sex, get emergency contraception.

If you're on the combined pill, missing just one pill anywhere in your pack, or starting the new pack one day late, is not a problem.

If you've missed up to two pills, anywhere in the pack (or just one if you're on Loestrin 20, Mercilon, Sunya or Femodette):

- Relax. Take the last pill you missed now.
- Continue taking the rest of the pack as usual.
- No additional contraception needed.
- Take your 7 day break as normal.
- You don't need emergency contraception.

If you've missed three or more pills (two if taking the pills Loestrin 20, Mercilon, Sunya or Femodette):

- Relax. Take the last pill you missed now.
- Continue taking the rest of the pack as usual.
- Leave any earlier missed pills.
- Use an extra method of contraception for the next seven days.
- If you have had unprotected sex in the previous few days, get emergency contraception.

If seven or more pills are left in the pack after the missed pill(s):

- finish the pack have the usual seven-day break or take the placebo tablets.

If less than seven pills are left in the pack after the missed pill(s):

- **finish the pack and begin new one the next day (this means missing out the break or not taking the dummy tablets).**

FOR ANY PILL: If you miss pills in this month's packet, and have also missed pills in your previous packet, you may need emergency contraception or a pregnancy test.

If you aren't sure what to do (very common), continue to take your pill and use additional contraception, such as condoms, and seek advice.

NOTE: Remembering what to do about missed pills is so hard that many doctors get it wrong. I usually have to look it up. There should always be instructions in your pill packet but we should be teaching this at school. It's maths, biology, sociology, psychology, time management, future problem solving and communication skills in one riveting lesson. Master this and you can rule the world.

WARTS AND ALL

I once worked for a sexual health consultant who would take me out to lunch and talk about Chlamydia very loudly in a crowded room. And good for him. The first step in destigmatisation is to get it on the menu at Starbucks.

If I had a dose, would I know?

Probably not. The commonest symptom of a sexually transmitted infection is no symptoms at all. So not only do many people not realise they have one, but if it suddenly makes an appearance in

151

the middle of a relationship it does not prove infidelity. Some infections, like herpes, can take years to surface. If you start getting into a pointless, blame game, your relationship could tailspin.

What's a morning drop?

A milky drop that emerges from the tip of the penis when you get up in the morning. If it's white or clear but you're not sexually excited, then it's not semen. If it's yellow or green, it's definitely not semen no matter what time of the day it is, or what sort of erection you have. Put it away and get down to your nearest sexual health clinic. It can be sorted and although some discharges appear to go with time, they just sit tight as you pass it onto others, and they can spread up to your balls, prostate and even joints (a disaster if you're keen on sport). Professional careers have been ruined for want of a course of antibiotics.

What's the difference between an STD and an STI?

Only the name. Sexually transmitted 'diseases' were renamed 'infections' to sound less threatening. Some people call them sexually 'shared' infections, to promote the idea that very few people pass them on purpose, and usually it's impossible to say who had it first and for how long. Sex is all about sharing. If you share pleasure, there's a risk you'll share infection and it's essential that you share treatment. And when you have, you can please each other again and again, preferably with a fresh condom each time.

What's the difference between a clap clinic and a sexual health centre?

The clap clinics of twenty years ago were more properly called Genito-urinary Medicine (GUM) Clinics and had a ridiculous pseudonym to match, like 'the special clinic' or 'clinic 19' or 'Lydia.' They were generally buried in the back and beyond and because nobody knew what genito-urinary meant, and nobody could remember the pseudonym. The only patients who got treated were those brave enough to ask for directions to the clap clinic.

Modern sexual health centres are far easier to find, both by name and location, all prescriptions are free, your notes stay within the clinic and are not passed onto anyone, nor placed on any central computer database. You get testing and treatment for all sexual problems, advice about safe and healthy sex, counselling, contraception and sometimes even coffee. Just about every problem can be helped, if not cured. And there are no umbrellas. So no reason not to get checked out.

What's the prettiest sexually transmitted infection?

A lot of infections and even cancers look much less scary under a microscope. One way of coming to terms with them is to have a peek up close so you can visualise what you're dealing with. Trichomonas vaginalis is my favourite STI, because it's quickly diagnosed, easily cured and the infection rate is declining, when just about every other STI is becoming more common. It's a single-celled creature that wobbles and rotates as it waves its four tiny antennae. Very entertaining down a microscope but it can irritate your parts; soreness, discharge and a nasty smell. However, it's sorted with a single dose of antibiotics (for you and all your partners)

153

Is herpes worth the hype?

No. Genital herpes is just cold sores on your bits. No picnic, but not the end of the world either. Herpes does far more psychological damage than physical, largely because of the media. The misinformation started with the launch of a drug, acyclovir, which curtails and prevents attacks. So far so good, but the company was keen to get its investment back as quickly as possible, and the best way to do that was to inflate the importance of herpes.

Acyclovir was discovered in 1974 and in the long run-up to its launch in 1982, the drug company Wellcome (now Glaxo SmithKline) put its marketing department into overdrive. The media took the bait, and *Time Magazine* took it twice, describing herpes as 'the new sexual leprosy' (1980) and 'the new Scarlet Letter' (1982).

Absolute bollocks. Herpes is only incurable in the same way chicken pox is incurable. The virus hangs round in the nerve roots and can (but usually doesn't) reactivate. When it does recur, each attack tends to be milder than the last and is often unnoticeable. We don't call children with chicken pox 'lepers', so why pick on herpes?

Herpes simplex virus comes in two types: type 1 typically causes cold sores around the mouth; type 2 causes sores in the genital area, but both can cross over. Up to sixty per cent of new genital herpes is type 1, passed on by oral sex. So a lot of people out there are having a lot of oral fun without realising they're passing anything on. Seventy-five per cent of those with herpes have only mild or non-existent symptoms so you often don't know you've got it or are shedding the virus.

Very few people pass on an infection deliberately, and blame is destructive. First symptoms can appear months or years after the initial infection, so a sudden crop of blisters does not mean infidelity. Seventy to eighty-five per cent of people, depending on their age, have antibodies to type 1 herpes. We've nearly all been infected, but only a few get symptoms.

Type 1 antibodies give you a lot of protection against the symptoms of type 2 infection, so if one person in a couple has genital herpes, and the other has a blood test showing antibodies to type 1, he or she is very unlikely to be troubled by type 2 infection, even if it occurs. If your partner has type 2 antibodies, even better.

For the few people who get recurrent, severe herpes, acyclovir works well to suppress attacks. It's now been around so long, has had a name change (aciclovir), and is cheap as chips. A whole month's supply costs the NHS just £9, though many doctors are reluctant to give it because they still think of the very expensive wonder-drug launched twenty-seven years ago and they don't know much about herpes. A lot of women treated for recurrent thrush have herpes.

If you want good advice and great support, go to the Herpes Viruses Association (HVA). Founded over twenty-five years ago to counter the herpes hype, the HVA has been a beacon of sanity, destigmatising cold sores wherever they occur and counselling, supporting and educating those with herpes and those who treat it. Unfortunately, the Department of Health has just cut its funding, so its survival depends on donations. The HVA is so valuable to patients, partners and health professionals that I became a patron.

Shortly after acyclovir was launched and herpes hype hit a peak, a study of 375 people with genital herpes found that half had suffered from depression, thirty-five per cent avoided intimate relationships, thirty-five per cent reported decreased sex drive, ten per cent gave up sex completely and fifteen per cent had suicidal thoughts. In the UK, it's largely been left to the HVA to fight the stigma of herpes, and many of its supporters are in long-term relationships thanks to the support and advice it

155

gives out. They're only cold sores, and they go away even without treatment. But without the HVA, the guilt would last a lot longer.

For further information and donations: www.herpes.org.uk/

Is the UK the genital wart capital of the world?

It may well be soon, but it so easily could have been different. Back in 2007, a vaccine called Gardasil was launched that protects girls and women who've yet to have sex from viruses that cause both cervical cancer and genital warts. Many countries snapped it up, but the UK sat on its hands and waited, and then – in 2008 – decided to go with a vaccine called Cervarix, which protects against cervical cancer only. It was a huge wasted opportunity, and I did my best in *Private Eye*, the *British Medical Journal* and *Trust Me, I'm (Still) a Doctor* to shout about it.

Genital warts are very common (100,000 new cases a year in England alone) and although they don't kill you, they can kill your sex life for a while, are fiddly and expensive to treat (£25 million a year), often reoccur and condoms offer only partial protection. Choosing Gardasil, which has the same list price as Cervarix, would quickly save a lot of anguish and money

In Australia, they take genital warts seriously. Since April 2007, they've offered Gardasil to 12-18-year-old girls in a school-based programme, and it's also widely available to those not in school. By the end of 2008, researchers at the country's largest sexual health centre in Melbourne found a forty-eight per cent decrease in genital warts in women aged under twenty-eight years, and a seventeen per cent wart reduction in heterosexual men. This has resulted in substantial savings and freeing up of time to treat other sexually transmitted infections. Their biggest worry is that unvaccinated backpackers from places like the UK will spread genital warts in Oz, and it's even been suggested (hopefully in jest) that travellers should have to prove they've had Gardasil to gain entry.

Mass vaccination and patient choice don't sit easily together. Some parents, quite reasonably, may want to wait until more safety data is available before vaccinating their daughters, some may want to choose Cervarix because they think it might offer longer term protection against cervical cancer than Gardasil.

Everyone needs up-to-date, unbiased information to allow them to reach a conclusion. When I was researching Gardasil for my daughter, neither the NHS 'Choices' website nor the NHS vaccination website returned a single hit. Having made the choice for you, the government wouldn't even admit the possibility of an alternative. Those running the vaccine programme at my daughter's school hadn't even heard of Gardasil, they weren't allowed to give it and neither was our GP. Plenty of private clinics were offering it, for £400 and three trips into Bristol.

When the NHS is a bit shit, doctors phone their friends. I spoke to two sexual health consultants, both of whom advised I would be 'mad' not to protect my daughter against genital warts if I could, and one sent me a prescription for Gardasil. At a conference, Dr David Salisbury – head of the UK government's vaccination programme – dismissed my campaign for girls to be at least offered the choice of Gardasil and referred to me as 'the comedian and doctor.' I'd rather be a comedian and doctor than have all those genital warts on my conscience. Follow the link below, Dave. It's not very funny. www.chestersexualhealth.co.uk/genitalwarts.htm

Can you remove genital warts with a cheese grater?

You can, but other treatments are available. It's amazing the extent to which some people (particularly men) will avoid a trip to the sexual health clinic, using pipe cleaners, sandpaper, cigarette burns, detergent and even Domestos down the hole. The damage done by DIY is far worse than any infection.

Genital warts can be hard or soft, occur singly or in groups (and sometimes whole communities, like a floret of broccoli). They often cause no symptoms at all, other than difficulty in wiping or altered aim. But they can itch, bleed and make you very wary of showing your genitals or anus to anyone. And if pregnancy wasn't hard enough, warts often appear for the first time then.

Sexually transmitted infections like to hang out together so if you've got warts (or any other STI), you may well have something else so it's worth having some more tests. As with herpes, most people have encountered one of the thirty or so human papilloma viruses that can cause genital warts, but only the unlucky ones show signs of it. Like verrucas, treatment needs to be repeated, either with lotions or freezing. Don't put your penis in the freezer overnight or use the verruca gels you buy over the counter. The drugs you need are prescription only (Podophyllotoxin or Imiquimod.) And the freeze-thaw-freeze of cryotherapy needs an expert aim.

Treatment can be uncomfortable and the virus isn't completely eradicated, so thirty per cent of people have recurrences. On a brighter note, most people develop immunity as they get older, and if you've had Gardasil, you'll have immunity from the start. (**BORING FACT:** Smoking probably makes your warts last longer and in women increases the risk of cervical cancer . . . if you needed another reason to stop.)

Does Chlamydia make a good Christmas present?

No but it's as common as socks. As sexual health consultant Peter Greenhouse puts it: 'If you haven't got Chlamydia by thirty, you haven't been trying hard enough.' As with many infections, you don't often have any symptoms, which is why Chlamydia can cause damage under the radar. It is the commonest bacterial, sexually transmitted infection and the good news is that treatment is simple and nearly always successful. If isn't treated, the consequences can sometimes be devastating, especially for women. The bacteria can gradually spread up from the cervix to the fallopian tubes between the ovary and womb, where they destroy the fine 'hairs' responsible for wafting eggs down the tubes. The damage can lead to ectopic pregnancy (where the embryo develops in the tubes), infertility and pelvic inflammatory disease.

A common symptom in women is bleeding in the middle of the cycle because the cervix is inflamed. Even more common is not to have any symptoms, so the only way to know if you've got Chlamydia is to get tested. The tests are really simple and accurate – women can do their own vaginal swab; blokes just pee in a pot and you can ask to have the results texted to you if you like. In the UK, anyone aged fifteen to twenty-four is offered annual Chlamydia screening for free, without needing to be examined and the results aren't announced in school assembly. To find out where to get a test, go to www.chlamydiascreening.nhs.uk/ or phone 0800 567 123.

Chlamydia is more common in those under twenty-five but the effects of untreated infection can hit you much later. Thirty years ago, doctors in liberal Sweden recognised the dangers of Chlamydia by screening for the disease, educating the public and tracing and treating the contacts of those infected. The incidence of pelvic inflammatory disease fell to a sixth of its former level. In Britain, research into Chlamydia has been starved of resources and screening came in much later. We may have pioneered IVF, but if just a fraction of the resources had been channelled into preventing infertility instead, far fewer women would have need for it, and those who did might get it fairly.

Can you get crabs on your eyebrows?

Yes. And eyelashes, moustache and any hair that isn't too dense (chest, armpit, thigh and, of course, pubes) The French, who are very good at not making a fuss over such trifles, call crabs 'papillons d'amour' or butterflies of love. As in 'Ooh look. You've got a butterfly of love on your moustache. How sweet!'

Crabs can't hop, skip or jump, so they'll be no use in the Olympics. They can't fly or swim either. They hide in bushes, get from one person to another by bodily contact and are remarkably hardy (they've been found on 4,000-year-old mummies)

Crabs itch, especially at night and at 2mm across, they're just visible to the keen eye. If you think you've spotted one, catch it and look at it under a magnifying glass. All the legs emerge from the front of the body but the clincher is the middle and hind legs which have pincer-like claws. Hence the name.

Crabs are the ultimate idlers. They cling onto hairs and hardly move during daylight, transferring to another hair at night. You can buy a lotion such as Derbac M over the counter. Apply over the whole body from the neck down even if only your pubes are itching. Don't put it on your eyebrows or use it if you're pregnant. The lotion stays on overnight and if you repeat in seven days, you should take out any newly hatched eggs. Putting underclothes and bed linen through a hot wash is worth a shout too.

If you want the opinion of a crab expert, you want screening for other infections or you want a free prescription, go to a sexual health clinic. If you're feeling brave, ask to see the full glory of a magnified crab.

5

Body talk

Can you really die of embarrassment?

Yes. Cancer can pop up in the most embarrassing places but the sooner you seek help for blood, lumps, sores, pain or weight loss, the better. Many cancers are now curable but only if you come forward to be cured. I once met a man who let his testicle swell to fifteen centimetres – larger than a grapefruit – because he was embarrassed at having a lump down there and, as it got bigger, he was worried that his GP would think he was an arse for sitting on it for so long. It wasn't until it really pressed on the nerve endings that he sought help. He survived his cancer but lost a testicle that might well have been saved if he'd come earlier.

The cycle of delay caused by embarrassment, fear, stoicism and misplaced optimism is common throughout medicine. It causes huge suffering and occasionally death, and isn't always easy to predict. Some people are ashamed at having a dose or shy about revealing a breast lump or rectal bleeding. Dandruff, warts, halitosis, prominent ears, acne, burst condoms, incontinence, dribbling, man boobs, excessive sweating, hairiness, impotence, cotton buds stuck in the ear, golf clubs stuck in the rear . . . just about any problem you care to name, someone's delayed getting help for fear of the reception.

Receptionists are much friendlier than they used to be and doctors and nurses should be beyond embarrassment. We've seen it all. At least twice. These days I only turn pink after sex or if I fall asleep in the sun (hence the nickname Salmon Hammond). Check it out on a website first (www.embarrassingproblems.com is a good start), then go and show it to a doctor. Or that nice smiley nurse.

Do I have to lie on my left-hand side, draw my knees up to my chest and take a few deep breaths?

No. Seeing a doctor with an anal problem (yours not his) is generally far more embarrassing for you than him. He (or she) will have heard about and seen dozens of anuses and shouldn't be the least bit fazed. He should listen to your story and acknowledge your concerns before leaping in with the gloves and jelly. You can take a friend in with you (choose wisely) or ask to have a chaperone present. If you don't want to be examined, it's fine to say so. If you don't want to be examined on your side, tucked up and facing the wall you could ask to try standing up and leaning forward.

Slow deep breathing with your mouth open helps relax your sphincter enough to allow a finger in, and with a gentle approach and plenty of lubrication, it should slip in quite easily. We start by parting the buttocks slightly to look around the opening for piles, tags, warts or cracks in the anal wall. Then the fingertip is pressed gently at the anal opening until it relaxes and in we go. It's not unheard of for the end of the doctor's tie to slip in too, but that's generally a mistake you only make once. Hopefully, you also throw that particular tie away. Doctors probably shouldn't wear ties at all – they carry all sorts of germs and the visual image of a doctor sweeping a tie over his shoulder prior to an intimate examination can stay with you for life.

It's quite hard for us to see your face in either position, so if it's painful say so. We tend to rotate the finger once it's in to feel all around. One of my consultants used to say: 'If you don't put your finger in it, you'll put your foot in it.' He wasn't being literal, but pointing out that a rectal examination is very useful for picking up rectal and prostate cancer. Sometimes a bit of poo pops out on the glove, but that's actually quite useful for us to check if there's any blood in it. Then it's a quick wipe, a chat about the findings and a trip to the loo or the nurse on the way out if you need to offload.

FOR HIM
Can you check your own prostate?

In theory, yes, but you need a long finger and some lubrication, leaning slightly forward in the shower. The prostate can be felt through the front wall of the rectum and is normally quite smooth and a bit squidgy (although not unpleasantly so). It has a central groove and should be roughly the same size either side. Any hard lump or obvious asymmetry needs checking out, although it isn't always cancer. Now wash your hand. Some American websites advocate self-examination of the prostate but I've never met a man who's admitted it. Most don't even get as far as their testicles.

If you want to do a fingerless check-up, search Google for the International Prostate Symptom Score. It's a great game to play down the pub when they've lost the cribbage board. All the questions are about your bladder habits over the last month. I've paraphrased slightly:

- **How often have you had a sensation of not emptying your bladder completely after you thought you'd finished?**

- How often have you had to urinate again less than two hours after the last time?
- How often have you found you stopped and started several times during a performance?
- How often have you found it difficult to hold out against the desire to pee?
- How often have you had to push or strain to get the party started?

Score each of these either 0 (not at all), 1 (less than 1 time in 5), 2 (less than half the time), 3 (about half the time), 4 (more than half the time), 5 (almost always). The bonus question, for which you're allowed to phone your wife, is: Over the last month, how often did you typically get up to pee during the night from the time you went to bed to the time that you normally get up? (Score a mark each).

There's clearly an element of subjectivity here, but 20 or over is a very high score (and anything over 9 is worth sharing with a doctor). If you need some tie-breakers, try 'where is your prostate?', 'what does it do?', 'how does it interfere with your flow?' and 'where's that bloody cribbage board?'

A doctor may want to do the finger thing, even if you've done it yourself, and you may be referred for uroflowmetry. It sounds technical but it just measures how quickly you pee into a pot. You can do this at home (or in the pub, but probably best in the gents, or at least the snug.) You need a measuring jug and a stopwatch. (**NOTE:** A lot of men suffer from bashful bladder, and so a grand pee-off along the urinal may confuse those who have prostate problems with those who are just shy.)

Here's what you're measuring:

- Start to finish times for actual peeing and trying to pee but nothing much happening;
- The volume of pee;
- The time it takes for you to get into full flow;
- Divide your pee volume by your flow-time to get your average speed.

Like a fast car, a young man should hit top acceleration within seven seconds and offload around 400 mls in twenty seconds. Anything consistently under 250 mls or over 75 seconds suggests a hold up. As does someone knocking on the door and asking 'are you alright in there?'

Uroflowmetry has a couple of advantages over DIY. It measures the peak flow-rate (anything over 15 ml/sec is very good, but hard to accurately judge yourself unless you switch to a second jug for your best second). Also it's less likely to interfere with the baking.

If all this is a bit anal, just consider how much your peeing is pissing you off. If it causes you discomfort, embarrassment, annoyance and marital conflict, and stops you doing something you might enjoy (e.g. going to a football match), then get it checked. Either drugs or surgery (or both) can make a huge difference. The same applies to women (not the prostate bit, obviously, but the getting help for leaking or dribbling. It happens to most people who've pushed out a nine-pounder or two).

Is it possible to have a prostate examination without getting an erection?

Yes. Some men enjoy prostate massage as part of their daily routine, or perhaps just a special treat on high days and holidays, but in a medical setting, the digital assessment of prostate size with you lying on your side, knees tucked up and trying not to fart doesn't seem to reach the erection centre of the brain. And if it did, the doctor is generally too preoccupied or polite to notice.

Is it true that tomato ketchup reduces your risk of prostate cancer and how should I apply it?

There's some evidence that two or more servings a week of red fruits containing lycopene – tomatoes, watermelons, red grapefruit and guava – can reduce your risk of prostate cancer by up to a quarter. The even better news is that you take them orally. Cooked or processed tomatoes are even more lycopene-rich and ketchup is an excellent sauce source (although it can be heavy on the sugar and salt). Oily fish three times a week has an even more impressive effect (up to forty-five per cent in the lowering of risk) but generally only Inuit people eat that much. Other possible prostate fillips include selenium (in grains, fish, meat and poultry), soy products and vitamin E.

Is dribbling a sign of prostate cancer?

It never used to be. When I trained, I was taught that cancer occurred towards the outside of the gland (and could often be felt with a finger) and benign enlargement occurred in the centre, pressing on the urethra as it passes through and causing dribbling/poor stream/stains on light summer trousers/getting up three times a night/separate bedrooms and eventually divorce. Not benign at all, really.

We now know that up to fifteen per cent of cancers also occur in this middle zone, so if you take your dribbling to the doctor (which is a good idea, because there are drugs that can help), she may well suggest a PSA blood test to assess the risk of cancer (either before or after the finger, depending on what sort of day she's having).

Is there anything more painful than a prostate biopsy?

Yes. A prostate biopsy without anaesthetic. And probably childbirth, though it's rare to endure both. Prostate biopsy is generally suggested for those who have suspicious finger-findings or a raised PSA blood test. It's done when you're fully conscious, but make sure they put a large squirt of local anaesthetic in first and give you antibiotics before and after to reduce the risk of infection. You'll also need a bit of time for the anaesthetic to kick in.

A well-equipped hospital will have an automatic biopsy gun guided by a transrectal ultrasound probe (yes, it goes in through the anus again). Around 8–14 biopsies are taken, depending on the size of your prostate, and – not having had the procedure myself – I only have patient accounts to go on. Some men find it bloody painful, some find it mildly uncomfortable. I suspect the difference lies both in the anaesthetic and the technique. If the doctor has trouble getting the gun out of the holster, ask if he's done it before. Or just grit your teeth and remember: Most men who have the biopsy don't have cancer.

How can I tell if my prostate cancer is a pussycat or a tiger?

Other than naming it yourself, we don't yet know which cancers will just curl up in your prostate, purr and do you no harm at all, and which will go on the rampage. We know from post-mortems that eighty per cent of men who reached eighty years of age had a pussycat cancer in their prostate that never did them any harm at all. On the other hand, tiger cancers are second only to lung cancer as a killer of men over fifty.

We are slowly getting better at telling the pussies from the tigers. How quickly your PSA blood level changes over time is helpful, and there's a new molecular marker called PCA3 measured from cells in the urine that seems to be a more specific and sensitive marker than the PSA test (which was once dubbed 'Promoting Stress and Anxiety' because it isn't that accurate). The downside of PCA3 is that you have to collect the urine sample immediately after a prostate massage, so you'll need a full-ish bladder, a willing health professional, a sense of humour and a pot to hand. Other genetically based tests are apparently in the pipeline.

Does anyone else have a hole on the underside?

Yep. 1 in 300 men are born with a penis hole in the wrong place (hypospadius), usually on the underside. If it's picked up in childhood, it can be completely sorted by a specialist (i.e. someone who does a lot of penis reconstruction, rather than someone just having a go). But it's not uncommon for parents to miss it and boys to get used to peeing on the floor or sitting down to pee. And because men don't generally compare penises with each other or ask a doctor to check it over, it's often a woman who just happens to be down that way who spots things aren't quite right. As an adult, a repair is still possible but may not be essential, depending on exactly where the hole is and whether you've got a funny foreskin or a bent shaft too. Ask your GP to refer you to a specialist who can show you before and after photos.

Oh, and if a friend ever asks: 'Does anyone else have a hole on the underside?', don't pretend you didn't hear or laugh or make him show you in the middle of a crowded bar. Just direct him to a GP or to this page.

What makes a bladder bashful?

At least one in ten men find it hard to pee with others looking on (even if it's sideways from ten feet away). The longer the queue, the more the performance anxiety kicks in and the less chance you'll get a cubicle because of all the other poor sods with bashful bladders in search of privacy. The longer you loiter at the urinal, the longer the sideways glances, until you give up and sit through the second half in torture (or nip out half way through, and miss the only goal of the game).

Researchers have shown, in a rather dubious experiment, that if you put a stranger next to you when you pee, it inhibits most men (more so, the closer the stranger gets). Family seem to have a less inhibitory effect (unless it's your mother-in-law or you discover that your teenage son now has a larger penis than you do). According to *The Lancet*, mammals mark their territory by urinating and leaving a scent, and some men subconsciously worry that peeing in the presence of another man asserts supremacy over his territory and challenges him to a fight. In my experience, this only happens if you piss on someone by mistake.

The cures are fairly obvious. Deep breathing, doing mental arithmetic or pretending you're a miniature man crawling around the cracks in the toilet tiles. Works for me.

Can you still write 'cello scrotum' on a sick note?

Not any more. After 'bad back' and 'a bit of a bug', cello scrotum was until recently my top sick note diagnosis. It was first described in 1974 by Dr (and now Baroness) Elaine Murphy as an addition to 'guitarist's nipple', a mild irritation caused by the rubbing of the instrument against the upper torso after vigorous plucking. If a guitar can chafe up above, why not a cello down below? In 2009,

Baroness Murphy admitted that the condition was a hoax; just a bit of a joke. But not for the thousands of people who've lived with the condition for thirty-four years.

As anyone who's owned a cello can tell you, you'd need a highly unusual playing position (or a very large hernia) to cause abrasion down below, but it is possible to cause a freak 'kebab' injury by slippage of the spike on a cold tile floor. Most of the people I've labelled with cello scrotum over the years don't possess a cello. Or even a scrotum. But the point about diagnostic labels is that they aren't just there to make a diagnosis but to help the recipient luxuriate in the full glory of the sick role. Just as a lot of people who develop tennis elbow don't play tennis and most of those with clergyman's knee aren't clergymen, we use a fancy diagnosis to spice up a boring one and big up the suffering. If you come to me with a sore shoulder, and I say 'you've got a sore shoulder', what use is that? But if I label you with 'pitcher's cuff', you've got out of sex, work and the washing up for a fortnight.

My cello-chafing days may be over, but I shall continue to diagnose athlete's armpit (fungal infection of the pit, usually in very rotund non-athletes), farmer's bum (piles), fish fancier's finger (bacterial finger infection caught from tropical fish nibbling) and even chimney sweep's scrotum. The latter was famously described by Percival Pott in 1775, and is a most unpleasant tumour caused by prolonged soot exposure. It's become much rarer now we no longer send small boys up chimneys but you'd be amazed what half an hour on the naughty step can do, especially if the carpet's a bit rough.

As for sick notes, they're on the way out too. These days, we're supposed to give out 'fit notes' instead, to accentuate what work you can still do. You may not be able to play the cello but you can still pluck a guitar. You may not be able to go up the chimney but that doesn't stop you from being a clergyman. All you have to do is believe.

Should foreskins be cut off willy-nilly?

No. It's odd that female circumcision is considered a barbarous abuse of human rights, but the male equivalent is seen by many as a mere trifle, and hardly worth getting worked up about. The foreskin is not a redundant quirk of evolution, but actually comprises between fifty and eighty percent of the penile skin (depending on the length of the shaft). If laid end to end, it would have over three feet of veins, arteries and capillaries and 240 feet of nerve fibres with 20,000 nerve endings. Unravelled, it measures 15-20 square inches and they've even developed a way of growing skins for burns' victims from the foreskins of circumcised baby boys. From each one, they can grow enough skin to cover six football pitches.

Personally, I'd still rather play on grass but it's clear there is far more to a foreskin than meets the eye. So what's it for? It expands to cover the shaft during sex, facilitates a smoother thrust and all those nerve endings make it more enjoyable. Not that circumcised men can't enjoy sex, they just have a bit less feeling at the tip. The foreskin also protects the head of the penis and has glands that aid lubrication and produce anti-bacterial proteins like those found in breast milk.

So why would anyone want to remove it? Good question. The first known drawing of a circumcision is on the wall of a Dynastic tomb in Egypt, which dates it at around 4,400 years old. It is still performed widely for religious reasons, for example, on eight-day-old baby boys in the Jewish faith, although Jews themselves have questioned the wisdom of doing it without anaesthetic.

In Israel, the custom of removing the foreskin after death prior to a Jewish burial has now been outlawed. In Western culture, non-religious circumcision became big business in the Victorian era to discourage masturbation (it only works in the short term) and as a 'cure' for insanity, epilepsy, hysteria, tuberculosis and

171

short-sightedness. In 1891, Jonathan Hutchinson, president of the Royal College of Surgeons of England, wrote an article entitled 'On Circumcision as a Preventative of Masturbation', in which he wrote: 'Clarence was addicted to the secret vice practised among boys. I performed circumcision. He needed the rightful punishment of cutting pains after his illicit pleasures.'

By the turn of the century, amputation of the foreskin was 'scientifically proven' to cure and prevent malnutrition, paralysis, bed-wetting, hip-joint disease, headache, alcoholism, criminality, club-foot, and heart disease. Unbelievably bad science. Some recent studies have shown that circumcision may help prevent cancer of the penis and reduce the risk of sexually transmitted infections, but good personal hygiene, not smoking and having safe sex are far more important. We could cut lots of bits of our anatomy off if we couldn't be bothered to clean them properly or didn't want them to get infected or cancerous, but generally we leave them be and enjoy them. So why pick on the foreskin?

In America, the only country in the world to circumcise the majority of its sons without religious reason, the foreskin has truly become a fashion victim, and although rates have dropped form eighty-five per cent in the sixties to sixty per cent now, it's still big business in a recession. Some women believe that because circumcised men feel less they have more staying power, and that a circumcised 'regular guy' penis looks nicer, but this is hardly a reason to go chopping off half a man's penile skin. In Finland, where foreskins are valued, there is no removal at birth and the chance of needing a circumcision later on for a very tight, infected foreskin is just 1 in 16,667.

In the UK, we still remove thousands of foreskins a year for medical reasons but most of these could have been saved by other methods, such as the use of steroid creams to ease a tight ending and antibiotics for infections. Half of all medical circumcisions are performed in the under tens, and a third in the under six, with most religious circumcisions still done in the first few days of life. Some men feel angry that they were genitally mutilated as children without their consent, and deprived of a very useful part of their anatomy. As Dr John Warren, an outspoken champion of the foreskin puts it: 'Not having one is like listening to an orchestra without violins. Something is definitely missing.' There are some rare medical reasons for circumcision, such as a skin condition called BXO or a scarring and narrowing of the foreskin which makes it impossible to pull back, but aside from these, we should just keep it clean and let the foreskin be. If only that had been the Beatle's B-side.

Can I do my own circumcision?

I really wouldn't try. Circumcision is not just a simple snip, but a complex procedure that requires considerable skill. And the smaller the penis is, the easier it is to cut off more than you intended. Complications range from amputation of the entire penis, damage to the glans and urethra, haemorrhage, infection and poor cosmetic results. If anyone I loved genuinely needed one, I'd make sure it was done in hospital, under general anaesthetic, by an experienced paediatric surgeon.

Anaesthesia is rarely an issue in religious circumcision, most of which is done outside hospital on conscious newborn infants. Ritualistic circumcision is bad enough, but doing it without any form of analgesia is barbaric. Medical circumcisions are never justified under the age of three and rarely before five years. Religious circumcisions on newborns are especially risky as the penis is so small. They should only be performed with adequate pain relief and preferably when the child is old enough to choose whether he wants his penis skin cut off. Most, I suspect, would say no.

Can you regrow your foreskin?

Some men feel so incomplete after a circumcision that they attempt to regrow their foreskins with an elaborate system of taping and weights. This may provoke gales of laughter down the pub but if you type 'foreskin restoration' into your search engine, you'll be deluged with illustrated diaries testifying to its success. There are even entries from bemused, embarrassed but ultimately won-over wives. I would start at the NORM website (the National Organization of Restoring Men www.norm.org) where you can now download the restoration bible, *The Joy of Uncircumcising*, as an e-book.

Is it possible for a black man to have a pink penis?

Yes, if he's a coal miner who's popped home for lunch. There's also a condition called 'vitiligo' that causes the skin to lose its pigment and can occasionally affect the penis. There is no cure. Sunbathing makes it worse because the skin of the affected part has no melanin, so won't tan and is liable to burn very easily. On the plus side, there are some pretty good camouflage creams around (they won't make your penis disappear) and even if you do nothing, it won't drop off. But whatever colour your penis has turned, it's always worth showing it to a doctor to confirm the diagnosis.

I've got scrotal swelling. Dr Google says it might be elephantiasis. What do you think?

I'd need to see your scrotum, preferably with you attached, but generally common things are common, and elephantiasis is very rare, especially in Somerset. Far more likely to be a fluid-filled sac (hydrocele) or a bag of worms (varicocele). Either way, you need to show it to a health professional soon. As our practice nurse puts it: 'When you hear hooves on a bridge, think first of a horse, not a unicorn.'

Can you check both testicles at once, to save time?

You can, but men aren't great at multi-tasking and there's a risk you'll spin them in opposite directions. Around 1,500 men develop testicular cancer each year in the UK, and it's the most common cancer in young men. The incidence has doubled in the last twenty years for some unknown reason, but it has a very good cure rate and your sex life and fertility are usually not affected. All you have to do is spot the lump and get help.

Examine your testicles during or after a shower or bath, when the scrotum is relaxed and the balls are hanging proud. Look for any swelling, and then roll the testicles, one at a time (or both if you're ambidextrous), gently between the fingers and thumb. They should feel smooth and rubbery. At the back and top of the testicle is the curly sperm tube (epididymis). Compare sides but, like breasts, it's not uncommon to have one slightly bigger than the other or one hanging lower (usually the left)

A cancer may start like a grain of sand on the surface of the testicle itself and then grow into a more obvious lump. Show any new lump or tenderness to your GP pronto. The sooner it's picked up, the easier the treatment.

Why do doctors lose interest in your testicles when you hit fifty?

Doctors become less excited by scrotal lumps when you hit fifty, because they're much less likely to be cancerous. However, there's plenty that can still go down in the ageing scrotum. One of the first slides I was shown as a medical student, was of a man pushing his scrotal hernia around in a wheelbarrow. It was prize marrow-sized and then some. Generally, anything approaching a melon will rekindle the interest pretty quickly.

FOR HER
What should I expect from an internal examination?

No surprises. The Royal College of Obstetricians and Gynaecologists has an 'Intimate Examinations Working Party', which convened in 1997 and then updated itself in 2001. Four members of the six-man party are women, and they have produced thirty-seven pages of guidelines for embarrassing examinations that you can download at the college website www.rcog.org.uk

In a nutshell, it's your body, no one can poke and prod you without your consent. You should be told what's being proposed and why, and you can opt out at any time. You should be treated with dignity, respect and a warm, gentle speculum, in private (but you can ask for a chaperone and a translator). If you would like a female doctor, they will try their best to arrange it. Examination banter should avoid anything jocular; no pet names, no commenting on suntans or through-draughts, and no discussing sexual response until the gloves are off.

Other guidelines worth knowing include:

- 'All sensible measures to reduce the extent and duration of nudity should be taken.'
- 'Gloves should be worn on both hands during vaginal and speculum examinations.'
- 'In the course of routine pelvic examination,

care should be taken to avoid digital contact
with the clitoris.'

- 'Every effort must be made to ensure that such
examinations take place in a closed room that
cannot be entered while the examination is
in progress and that the examination is not
interrupted by phone calls, bleeps or messages
about other patients.'

- 'There is no scientific evidence to support the
use of rectal examination as means of assessing
the cervix in pregnancy or labour and, as most
women find it more distressing than vaginal
examination, it cannot be recommended.'

- 'Fully informed written consent must be
obtained for all still or video photography. The
woman's privacy and modesty must be protected
and every effort must be made to ensure that
the video and photographic images have no
sexual connotations.'

- 'Informed consent must be obtained for any
intimate examinations that are undertaken
under anaesthesia. It is good practice for all
personnel in the operating theatre to treat the
patient with the same gentleness and respect
that they would apply were she awake, avoiding
personal comments and protecting the patient's
modesty wherever possible.'

The fact that the college has seen it necessary to articulate
what to many would seem blindingly obvious is because some
really bad stuff has happened in the past. It's rare but there will
always be the odd dodgy doctor or well-meaning emotional

cripple, and these guidelines should help you spot them and speak up. Be wary of any doctor with a missing glove.

Are bakers good at examining breasts?

Yes, although I wouldn't go to Warburtons for a second opinion. Breasts are active all the time, particularly during the fertile years when they have to be at the ready each month, in case of pregnancy. As a result, breasts change in consistency and general lumpiness throughout each cycle, which makes it very confusing if you're trying to check for lumps.

The best method (taught to me by a breast specialist, not a baker), is to raise your arms above your head and have a close look once a month, in a big mirror. If one breast has always been a different size or shape from the other, there's nothing to worry about. But any new differences, particularly dimpling or distortion of the skin or nipple, need checking out. Then, gently knead your breasts against your chest wall. Cancerous lumps generally feel very hard or irregular and need checking out urgently. Squidgy or soft lumps are rarely cancer, but are worth checking out if they don't move with your cycle.

Does a mammogram have to squeeze my breasts so hard?

Well, it was invented by a man. Women with larger breasts tend to find it more of a squash but all breasts are tender when compressed between two hard plates. More distressing is that, although mammograms pick up most cancers where a lump can already be felt, they only pick up about half of unfelt cancers. And they can suggest you've got cancer when you haven't.

But this is true of all tests. Even in the best hands, we miss some cancers and worry or even treat some patients unnecessarily.

The risks of getting breast cancer wrong are lessened if you have the triple assessment of a specialist opinion, imaging with X-rays/scans and a biopsy of the tissue.

Can I examine my ovaries?

Not easily. The ovaries are well tucked away and although your partner could theoretically check them out for you, in the same way that you might give his testicles the once over, just the thought of trying to locate the ovaries would send most men into meltdown. Which is why we have doctors.

The trick is knowing when to get your ovaries checked out and that's very hard. The symptoms of ovarian cancer can be vague and difficult to recognise early on, and when I trained I was told that ovarian cancer was 'a silent killer' and had no symptoms at all. This usually isn't true — it's just that the symptoms are not heard, or put down to something else, like irritable bowel or premenstrual syndrome. Persistent swelling in your stomach needs an urgent specialist referral.

Early symptoms of ovarian cancer may include:

- **pain in your pelvis, lower stomach, or side;**
- **a full, bloated feeling in your stomach;**
- **difficulty eating, or feeling full very quickly;**
- **needing to pass urine more urgently and frequently than normal.**

Later symptoms may include:

- **swelling in your stomach;**
- **pain in your lower stomach;**

- pain during sex;
- constipation;
- irregular periods.

Advanced symptoms (for any cancer) may include:

- nausea;
- weight loss;
- breathlessness;
- loss of appetite;
- tiredness.

If you think any of this could be you, get checked out (and particularly if a close relative had ovarian cancer). An internal examination awaits, and possibly blood tests, scans or scopes. It's a bugger to diagnose and treatment is no picnic, but the sooner it's picked up the better.

There is no national screening programme yet, but you may be eligible for screening if you have two or more close relatives (such as your mother, sister, or daughter) on the same side of your family, who had ovarian cancer diagnosed at a young age (under fifty years). See your GP.

Is there any way of making a cervical smear less embarrassing?

Women do their own Chlamydia swabs and I'm sure it won't be long before you do your own smears. I know one DIY nurse but it's probably still a bit fiddly for everyone to do it. Most women have an embarrassing smear story. In these days of targets, some doctors and nurses will try to spring a surprise smear on you when you've popped down with a tickly cough. You don't have to have one, and certainly not if you're wearing dodgy pants or hiding a strawberry. But you can if you want. Nurses aren't fazed by much. They'll even give you the strawberry to take home.

When I ask an audience for their smear experiences, women are surprisingly forthcoming. One spoke of freshening up with glitter spray by mistake, and presenting the GP with 'a night of a thousand stars.' Another told of the horror of being asked by an overly-smiley nurse to 'pop her little panties down and flop her legs like a frog.' And one woman became allergic to small talk after a nurse commented on the cut of her tunic during the smear, then sniffed and said: 'Oooh. That's a nice perfume.'

The trick with smears is to give some thought about how you'd like to be treated and let the nurse know. Do you like the cosy chat or do you prefer clinical silence? Would you like a chaperone? Do you prefer a warm or freezing speculum? If you want a GP to do a smear, don't slip it in at the end of the ten minutes. You'll be told to book a whole consultation. Not to be confused with a consultation for your hole.

Is cervical cancer a sexually transmitted infection?

No, but it can be triggered by one. Infection with certain types of human papilloma virus (HPV) can cause changes in the cervix which can one day lead to cancer. So there are various ways of reducing your risk of cervical cancer. One is to not have many partners. Another is to always use condoms no matter how many partners you have. Another is not to miss any cervical smears. Another is not to smoke, which seems to make it more likely for the damage caused by HPV to progress to cancer. And the newest way is to have a course of an HPV vaccine, which seems very effective at stopping the types of virus most commonly associated with cancer.

Currently, girls can get the HPV vaccine Cervarix free in the UK in a school-based vaccination programme (it's most effective if given before you've ever had sex). Outside of the programme you may have to pay, especially if you want the Gardasil vaccine which protects against both cancer and genital warts.

Why does my bra ride up my back?

Either because it's too big, it's come undone or you forgot to do it up in the first place. If it keeps happening, you either need a new bra or a visit to the memory clinic.

A surprising number of women wear bras that don't fit. And there are so many on the market, it's not easy to get the cups, shoulder straps, body straps, wires, under-wires, cross over wires, hooks and fastenings all in the right place . . . and look attractive. If yours wrinkles, squashes together, sticks up, digs in, bulges out, rides up, looks ridiculous or gives you back pain, treat yourself to a proper fitting with a bra specialist. I'm told it's a life-changing event for many women.

Should I wear crotchless pants to the doctors?

No thanks. They can shave a minute or so off a smear but they do send out the wrong message. As a naïve student (ginger hair, science A levels, not many girlfriends), I encountered my first pair of lady-gap knickers and assumed the owner must have snagged them alighting from her bicycle. Some male GPs claim to be thrown off-kilter by 'inappropriate underwear' but it's sometimes hard to judge what's acceptable. Will only pristine white cotton ones do? In an ideal world, any underwear exposed to strangers should pass the Daz doorstep challenge but sod's law of appendicitis is that when it flares up, you're always sporting pants that, in Jo Brand's immortal words, 'should have been buried at the bottom of the garden with a stake through them.'

After the menopause, do you just have to pad up and shut up?

No. But I'd hate to be a woman. Birth, babies, periods, work-life guilt, caring, cleaning, more periods with heavier bleeding, hot flushes, even hotter flushes and then finally, mercifully, the menopause. But can you relax? Can you buggery. Vaginal dryness and soreness, painful sex, leakage of urine and recurrent wee infections that don't respond to antibiotics. It doesn't happen to every woman but when it does, far too many suffer in silence.

So what's going on here? Women (and men) have oestrogen receptors all over their bodies and after the menopause, the lack of oestrogen is felt everywhere. Most women are aware of the hot sweats, emotional changes and longer term risks of osteoporosis, but symptoms down there are harder to talk about. Without oestrogen, the skin and support tissues of the vulval lips and vagina become thin and less elastic. This makes them more easily damaged, especially during sex if lubrication is poor. Even the everyday friction of your vulva rubbing against underwear can cause discomfort. And don't even try getting on a bike.

The oestrogen lack also changes the pH of the vaginal secretions, suppressing normal levels of good bacteria (e.g. lactobacilli) and leading to a watery, discoloured, slightly smelly discharge that can cause burning and irritation. Unsurprisingly, some women think they must have a sexually transmitted infection.

Lack of oestrogen also makes your pelvic floor sag, and many women get some prolapse as the womb drops down against a weakened vaginal wall (usually at the front). The hood that protects the clitoris can shrink, which can leave the clitoris sore, exposed and very difficult to talk about. And then there are the urinary tract symptoms, ranging from incontinence to an overactive bladder and recurrent symptoms of urinary tract infections.

Talk it through with a health professional who's likely to understand (say, a mid-fifties nurse. Don't see many of them). Soap tends to make skin dry, which is bad news for an already dry vagina, so switching to aqueous cream can make a difference. As for lubricants, the best well-known (KY Jelly) is a lot messier than Liquid Silk or Replens MD (available on prescription or over the counter).

Local oestrogen therapy can make a huge difference to vaginal dryness, soreness and urinary symptoms. It comes in the form of daily tablets, pessaries and creams, or a vaginal silica ring that can be inserted for three months. The good news is that the dose of oestrogen is low and the risk of side effects associated with HRT is much smaller. Pelvic-floor exercises are always worth doing, and there are even pelvic-floor physiotherapists who know all the tricks and tools to strengthen things up. Occasionally, surgery is needed for prolapse or stress incontinence (the kind that makes you leak when you cough or jump), but it's much less invasive than it used to be. For further information, *see* www.menopausematters.co.uk

INTERESTING FACT: After the menopause, women often have lower oestrogen levels than men.

Should I squeeze before I sneeze?

If you've got time, although sneezes can catch you unawares. There's loads that can be done for an unpredictable bladder, whatever the cause, and I find the nurse knows far more about it than any GP. One of ours gets women and their partners to tighten the anus and work the pelvic floor as if in a lift. You start in the basement and work your way up to the penthouse suite, and back down again. Incontinence needs a friendly ear and a correct diagnosis. Once you've got that, treatment quickly follows.

A teabag is good for vulval pain, but can I use it for tea first?

You can, but you need to let it cool off first. Teabags, particularly Indian or Earl Grey (for the posher vulva), contain tannic acid which is a local anaesthetic and can sooth the lower lips. You can either put teabags in the bath or apply a *cold* damp bag directly to the sore area.

Just as important is to get a correct diagnosis for your vulval pain. Genital herpes, especially the first attack, can be bloody sore and it can be painful or impossible to pass urine. You need more than teabags, you need a high dose of aciclovir (800mg three times a day), as soon as possible. If you catch it early, the worst may be over in just two days of treatment If you want an accurate diagnosis and a free prescription, a sexual health clinic is the place to be. *(See also* **Is herpes worth the hype?**).

A lot of people never get recurrences of herpes or get them so mildly they don't realise. But if you're one of the unlucky few who get severe recurrences, you can either have regular suppression treatment or learn to spot an attack early and nip it in the bud. The virus lives quite harmlessly in the spinal nerve roots, only causing pain when it travels down the end of a nerve. The commonest warning shot is a tingling sensation – could be in the lower buttocks, down the back of the legs to the knee, or round the backside. That's the time to take the tablets. Get them in time and you won't need to waste a teabag.

Other causes of a painful vulva are poorly understood so we give them a silly name. 'Vulval vestibulitis syndrome' is sudden pain, often right at the opening for no apparent reason, more common in young women. 'Vulvodynia' is more of an aching and itching, often worse at night, and more common in older women. The vulva looks normal but the pain isn't. And then there's cancer of the vulva which, like cancer of the penis, is rare but not something you'd want to sit on. Get it checked out.

Things to do with your vulva:

- Love it. It will get better in time.
- Use unperfumed soap, such as Simple.
- Wash your pants in 'sensitive' detergent.
- Put two handfuls of salt in your bathwater.
- Pee in the bath (it often helps the pain).
- Other things that some women find helpful include talking, listening, ice, aloe vera gel, aqueous cream, vitamin E oil (squeezed out from a capsule) and oatmeal (Aveeno) baths.
- Your GP can offer guidance on anaesthetic cream (which can safely enable you to have sex, if you want to try), prescription drugs for pain or referral to a vulval clinic.
- Contact the Vulval Pain Society www. vulvalpainsociety.org

Things not to do with your vulva:

- Give up.
- Get bubble bath, shower gel or shampoo near it.
- Use any deodorant down there, intimate or otherwise.
- Douche, shower or squirt anything into your

vagina. Like your ears, it cleans itself perfectly naturally (well, not quite like your ears but the point is, let it be).

- Get confused surfing – Americans say 'vulvar', not 'vulval', but they have some good sites too (e.g. www.vulvarhealth.org).
- Punish it.

How do you put yoghurt into your vagina without getting it all over the settee?

Putting live yoghurt over your vulva and into your vagina can relieve the symptoms of thrush, but may not make it go away any faster. If you want to have a go, the vulva is easy enough to cover but the vagina can be a bit awkward. A good way of getting it up high is to put a tampon in an applicator and leave a space at the top for yoghurt. Then pop it in the normal way, remembering to take it out again in an hour or so. If that doesn't work, there are plenty of thrush remedies available over the counter. You could just do it for the taste of yoghurt, but be wary of the whole-fruit pieces.

TO SHARE

Should I turn my belly button inside out to clean it?

No, that will only make it sore. If it's already sore or discharging, wash it gently with salty water and tenderly dab it dry. If the discharge doesn't go or turns yellow, show a nurse. If a baby comes out of it, you're dreaming or on mushrooms.

Should I pop piles back in with the end of my toothbrush?

Not with the brushing end. Haemorrhoids, like singers, usually come in three degrees. First-degree piles stay in the anus and generally don't trouble you, second-degree piles pop down when you have a poo but then pop back up again. Third-degree piles also pop down with straining but don't go back without a little help. Don't use anything as hard as a brush handle, just gently push them up with your finger while relaxing the sphincter. Now wash your hands. If you're really unlucky, you can get a fourth-degree pile that hangs around permanently. But she was never really part of the group and Dianna Ross won't talk about her.

Piles are derived from the Latin pila or ball, and strictly could apply to any roughly spherical swelling peeping through the anal verge (e.g. a misplaced walnut or a lost bearing). Haemorrhoid, on the other hand, is Greek for blood flow. Don't assume that bleeding coming from your rectum is due to piles. It probably is, but it's worth getting a medical opinion.

Piles are not varicose veins, but swollen, sponge pads. A healthy anus has three spongy pads (at 4, 7 and 11 o'clock around the margin if you're lying on your back with your legs in the air and a well-placed vanity mirror). These are like lips at the other end of your gut, and they act as an extra seal to keep the backdoor shut until the brain commands it to open. A pile is simply one of these soft pads that has slipped down (often through over-straining to pass a few hard pellets) and, as it slips, its blood vessels are compressed, making it swell up. This can result in an itching, aching, bleeding, tender lump and even skid marks if the seal goes. If the piles are up inside you, you may get painless, bright red drips of blood into the toilet, streaks on the paper or a coating of the stool (but not mixed in with it, which suggests bleeding higher up). External piles can bleed too, if a clot breaks through the skin. This is rarer and usually noticed as a stain on the pants.

Most of us get piles at some stage, as a punishment for evolving to walk upright (so things have a tendency to slip down). Piles can run in families and pregnancy, age, heavy lifting, heavy body, diarrhoea and constipation increase the risk. However, cold stone walls and hot radiators don't make piles more likely, just more likely that you'll feel them. They can go away on their own, particularly if you avoid the urge to scratch. The itchiness is down to a little lower bowel mucus leaking out and irritating the skin. Washing gently with warm, salty water, dab drying with cotton wool balls and a light smearing of petroleum jelly may be all that's needed to keep them in check.

Soft bog paper helps, or a bidet if you're posh, as do baggy pants, plenty of fibre and fluids and easy on the after strain. Piles can trick the body into thinking there's more to come when there isn't, so a swift drop off with no loitering is best. Laxatives and paracetamol are a good combination, and there are lots of soothing ointments and gels available over the counter. Some have unfortunate names like Anusol which — depending on how it's pronounced — can rather give the game away when shouted across a crowded dispensary.

Persistent third- or fourth-degree piles might need a little extra help. Most respond to putting a rubber band over the base until it falls off. It leaves a scar and it can cause soreness for forty-eight hours and bleeding, particularly if you're on blood-thinning drugs. But it sorts out the problem in eight out of ten cats. Old-fashioned haemorrhoidectomy is generally reserved for the really, really, really severe cases. Your legs are placed in the air and the piles are grasped with clamps and cut out with any accompanying skin tags all the way to the neck (of the pile, not you). On the upside, you do get a general anaesthetic for your trouble; on the downside, you need to be in hospital until your bowels have started working again which, according to my surgical textbook, may cause 'a certain amount of pain.' This is a euphemism for 'shitting a hedgehog backwards.' However, you get painkillers, laxatives and, if there isn't a staffing crisis, twice-daily baths to soothe the operation site and keep it clean. The wound may take four to six weeks to heal completely, during which time some discharge is normal. Newer methods, particularly removing the pile and stapling the skin edges back together, seem to have a quicker recover time.

Do piles strangle themselves?

Occasionally. Strangulated piles occur not for erotic pleasure but when a fourth-degree pile swells up, becomes very inflamed and then clots off. This can be so painful as to need urgent surgery. External haemorrhoids eventually shrink down to skin tags that make wiping a bit of a challenge, and may be excised.

Can I take my piles home with me?

You own your body parts, at least until you die, and if you ask nicely beforehand, you may be allowed to take them home for a formal burial. Or you may just get a look of bewilderment and a visit from the duty psychiatrist.

Can you catch threadworms by putting sticky tape over your anus?

You can catch the threadworms you already have, as they pop out of your anus at night and lay thousands of itchy eggs around the rim. You then scratch your arse, get the eggs under your nails and (later) put your fingers in your mouth, allowing the cycle of infection to repeat. Ingenious, really. As Dr Dog puts it: 'Never scratch your bum and suck your thumb.'

Threadworms are white, just over a centimetre long and

everyone gets them. You can get treatment over the counter (merbendazole), and are supposed to treat the whole family three times, a month apart, to cover any un-hatched eggs, as well as meticulous hand-washing, nail-clipping and separate bum towels. Or you can leave them be and hope they die out in six weeks.

What's the best cure for anal itch?

Don't scratch it. Wear loose pants and wash with water (only) after poos, dab dry, rub in a bit of aqueous cream but avoid soaps, disinfectants and deodorants. Some get relief from a cotton-wool ball dusted with baby powder and placed against the anus. The traditional remedy is to dab the dark star with the inside of a banana skin, but I've no idea who started that. King Kong, perhaps.

My GP said I could relieve my anal pain by sitting on a tennis ball. Shall I sue?

If he said it with a straight face, he probably thinks you've got proctalgia fugax, a ridiculous name masking the fact that we don't know why you're cramping up down there. The best guess is that it's a spasm of your rectal and pelvic-floor muscles, and if you're unlucky (and a man), you may get it after sex or even wake up at night with both the pain and an erection. It's hard to know what to do first in these situations. One tip that works for some is to put pressure on your perineum (the area between anus and genitals) by sitting on the edge of a bath or on a tennis ball. Don't try both – you're liable to slip off.

Some find a hot bath does the trick, others head for the ice. Drugs generally don't work because most cramps are over in the time it takes you to find them. If you get anal pain through a whole episode of *Eastenders*, it might be worth considering a prescribed drug to relax your smooth muscle. GTN spray (used for angina) or a salbutamol puffer (used for asthma), sometimes work if taken at the start of the pain. Failing that, it's two paracetamol and a mug of Horlicks (with or without the tennis ball). But you definitely don't need a lawyer.

Can you really burn your ear if someone phones when you're ironing?

Yes. Men are more likely to burn than women, partly because they're not used to ironing and partly because we find it hard to multi-task. We can iron or answer the phone, but not both at the same time.

I've only come across it once, in a sound engineer. I met him at a circumcision voiceover (enough said) and I spotted he was only using half his headphones. Some do this to look trendy. Others do it to allow the skin to re-grow.

He was cagey at first – as if being a sound engineer who can't differentiate between the hiss of a steam iron from the ring of a telephone was something to be ashamed of – but we gently managed to coax the truth out. Embarrassment is a very personal thing and often completely unjustified. An iron looks a lot like a phone, and he's not the first person to have made that mistake. He was too ashamed to visit a doctor, but the wound's healing well and all I could advise him was to take the phone off the hook next time he's ironing . . . or carving the turkey/stoking the fire/plunging the toilet.

The human and economic toll of accidents is vast. Seven and a half million people a year take their mishaps to casualty, including one in five of all the children in the UK. However, most are not a result of unlucky twists of fate, but rather ignorant, stressed or foolhardy Brits in a hurry. Which is why they're embarrassing. At school, there was a boy called Jack with no middle finger. He and his Dad were sorting out a very long string of Christmas lights and, without realising what the other was doing, they each put a plug on the end. Dad finished first, flicked the switch and you can guess the rest.

How much of my body should I shave?

As little as you can get away with. We're all African Apes and we're meant to be covered in hair. And no one ever said on their death bed: 'I wish I'd spent more time in electrolysis', or having a Brazilian, which I gather can be a touch painful, even in the best hands. Attempts at full-body stripping go in cycles of fashion, largely because women are made to think (by other women and manufacturers of hair-removal products) that men find body hair a turn off. Some probably do, but there are plenty who love a rim of lip hair and a forest of tight curls.

Back in the seventies, the bible of sexual fulfilment was *The Joy of Sex* by Dr Alex Comfort. The graphic line drawings were of a hirsute and strangely flexible man and his long-haired un-shaven companion. It contained fabulous advice such as:

> *Women used to chop off their armpit hair, or they did until a new generation realised it was sexy . . . In fact, the armpits should on no account be shaved, as they can be used instead of the palm to silence your partner at climax. If you must use your hand to clasp over his mouth, then make sure you rub it through the aromatic hairs in your own and your partner's armpit first.*

Sadly, the 2008 reprint of *The Joy of Sex* has lost much of the hair and the pit tip. But cut off all your hair and you're missing out on one of nature's finest aphrodisiacs. Where do you think musk comes from? I know it says 'extracted from the musk glands of Himalayan musk deer' on the bottle, but at least half of it is the sweat and smegma of any old hairy mammal. And a fine and enticing smell it is too. Sex expert Dr Ruth K. Westheimer is a keen advocate of armpit sex; a surprisingly enticing alternative when you fancy something a bit different, apparently, and all the better for a clump of moist, sweaty hair. You can't get pregnant that way but you'd be wise to use a condom in a pandemic, when those caught short without a tissue sneeze into their armpits. If swine flu and Chlamydia mix, we're all going down.

Shaving or hot waxing the genitals is now de rigueur for a generation brought up on a diet of hairless porn. Men and boys do it in the hope they'll look an inch longer, women I'm not so sure about. Some claim it makes the vulva easier for a man to find his way around but the pre-pubescent look is deeply disturbing. Pubic hair is nature's buffer for the bump and grind of life, and to remove it all can make sex uncomfortable. Plus, you end up with shaving rashes and nicks that take ages to stop bleeding, and look ridiculous with little squares of tissue paper on them. Every bush occasionally needs a back comb or a trim but genitals were not made to be stripped, buffed and polished.

Body hair removal is time-consuming, expensive, un-comfortable, unnatural and embarrassing (as any man who's had his 'back, sac and crack' done will testify). Life is all about difficult choices. If you're in a relationship, ask your partner if she'd prefer you to spend your disposable cash on the new-you eunuch look, or a nice meal out, followed by four hours of armpit sex. When did you last celebrate the joy of hair?

Can black pudding mimic the signs of bowel cancer?

Yes, and at both ends. The congealed pig's blood in black pudding can mimic human blood in your stool, in a well-known chemical screening test called the Faecal Occult Blood or FOB. This is the one where you have to collect a small dollop of your poo from pan or paper and smear it on a card. If it changes colour, you've got blood in your stool, either your own or your pudding's.

Do I have to have been to public school to find bowel screening acceptable?

No. But when FOBs were first trialled it was noticeable that those who'd had the benefit of a private education were more at ease with collecting and smearing their poo. However, it's actually very easy to do and, because bowel cancer is so common (it happens to one in twenty of us, and 16,000 people still die every year from it), it's worth trying to pick it up early. The NHS currently offers FOB screening automatically to everyone aged 60–69 every two years, and to anyone over 70 if you phone the helpline and ask for it (0800 707 60 60).

Why do I smell?

Because everyone else does too. In my teens, I read a Monty Python manual (easily the best source of medical information) that had a whole page on body odour. There was a self-help feature on better foreskin hygiene ('It pays to look after your penis'), a quiz ('Which vaginal deodorant does Cliff Richard use?') and a song to help break that awkward news to someone you love ('Honey, you smell').

We all have our own idiosyncratic tincture, often so faint

that it can only be detected by those who rub up against us. A few unfortunates give out signals at six feet, but whether or not these are deemed unpleasant depends on cultural norms as much as wind speed. What's not acceptable in Kidderminster could be flavour of the month in Kettering.

If you believe Darwin, there has to be an evolutionary advantage to smelling or it would have been chlorinated out of the gene pool. The female Emperor moth (*Eudia pavonia*) puts out a pheromone that can be picked up by a male 6.8 miles away, and its survival depends on it. No smell, no baby Emperors. For humans, it's probably got something to do with keeping the flies off your tucker or tracking your partner down in the dark. Perhaps it encourages us to mate with the same species. Some couples admit to finding each other's scent a turn on, but then sex has a remarkable capacity to make erstwhile vile smells and tastes alluring (if only for ten minutes.)

So, what actually causes us to smell? Sweat itself is largely blameless, unless you've pigged out on garlic, onions, curry and alcohol (hence the Sunday morning stinker). It's the colonisation of sweat that's been hanging around for several hours by chemical-releasing bacteria that's the problem. Sweat tends to congregate in areas from where it can't escape in polite society (genitals, nipples and armpits). These areas are also blessed with a special type of sweat gland, the apocrine gland, which produces sticky, milky fluid containing fats and proteins. These glands become active in adolescence and their fluid is said to be pheremonal. Unfortunately, it's also a bacterial feast. The other type of sweat gland (eccrine), is mostly concentrated on your forehead, palms and soles. Socks, gloves and woolly pom-pom hats provide an enclosed, airless environment for sweat-rotting bugs.

Clearly, if we didn't sweat, we wouldn't smell, but it's essential to control body temperature and stop you overheating. The average torso boasts two million sweat glands which churn out over three litres every twenty-four hours (2.1 mls a minute). Most of it evaporates easily. Hot weather, alcohol, exercise, obesity and agitation up the production, and humid conditions slow down evaporation. Some people sweat buckets even when they're cold, sober, slim, stationary and stress-free. Although upsetting, this isn't harmful unless it's combined with other symptoms which suggest something else is responsible, e.g. weight loss, weakness, trembling, increased appetite and bulging eyes (over-active thyroid gland or orgasm), night sweats, cough and weight loss (infection or tumour) or irregular periods (menopause)

So, how can you cut down on BO? The text-book advice to wash all over and change your pants, socks and any skin-hugging clothes every day seems condescending in the extreme. However, only a third of men wash behind their foreskin every day, while the majority are either too lazy or just enjoy their own smell. Some people with scrupulous personal hygiene still seem to sweat or smell excessively, and accusing them of skimping on the soap isn't particularly helpful. Others lack the mobility to reach under their armpits or perhaps can't afford the hot water. Using an anti-bacterial or anti-septic soap, particularly in your apocrine areas can help, but avoid over-washing as it can remove healthy skin bacteria and make the problem worse. It's a good idea to dry carefully after bathing and pamper yourself with talc as bacteria prefer moist skin. Tight or synthetic clothes and night garments are out; go for baggy cottons that allow the sweat to evaporate and sleep in the raw. Shower promptly after exertion, wear cotton socks, rotate your shoes round, go easy on alcohol and try not to pile on the pounds.

Deodorants alone just mask the smell and don't cut down on sweat rot. Choose wisely; the heady mix of BO and cheap perfume can be worse than BO alone. Go for one containing an antiperspirant too. These work by either stopping the bacteria from rotting or, rather perversely, by preventing the sweat from evaporating and holding the sweat and smell in. Experiment with a few to find which type and method of delivery suits you best. Some can cause irritation and you'd be unwise to apply them to broken skin or your genitals.

If this doesn't work, your doctor may prescribe a strong antiperspirant containing aluminium chloride. This reduces the amount of sweat you produce, but tends to cause skin irritation. Some people sort the smell but still get great lakes under the arms. In extreme cases, you can have the sweat glands surgically removed. Or just wear black shirts.

6
Forbidden fruit

Some of these questions are ridiculous and some are very rude indeed, but they're all my fault for suggesting 'there's no such thing as a stupid question.' Gonad games are a gas, so long as you know when to stop. Be gentle, take your time and always pause to consider: 'Am I rimming responsibly?'

GAMES PEOPLE PLAY
Can you have sex in a body scanner?

It's a tight fit, and there's no room to laugh, but it has been done before. Dutch researchers (who else?) at the University Hospital in Groningen invited couples to copulate inside their very expensive Nuclear Magnetic Resonance machine: a) to see if it was possible; and b) to see what happens to the genitalia in amazing detail. And, for the icing on the cake, they asked three single women to masturbate alone.

This is, I should point out, legitimate research and the pictures have been published in the *British Medical Journal* rather than *Dirty Wet Wipes* (although they may get the sell-through rights). Actually, the photos aren't horny at all but really rather unnerving. I doubt very much if the 'midsagittal image of the sexual response of a multiparous woman in the pre-orgasmic phase' will ever grace the *Pirelli* calendar. So why bother?

The researchers claim to have got the idea back in 1991 when they saw a scan of what happens to the throat of a professional singer when he sings 'aaa.' Then they remembered Leonardo da Vinci's epic drawing The Copulation (1493), which depicts all the inside bits during vertical copulation.* Was he accurate in his sketching? Clearly not, since in his view, the semen comes down from a man's brain via a channel in the spinal chord. Nice try, but no banana.

Talking of which, da Vinci drew the penis going in relatively straight, whereas our researchers found that 'during intercourse in the missionary position the penis has the shape of a boomerang and a third of its length consists of the root of the penis.' It's worth remembering this when faced with a penis that doesn't look much from the outside – it could just have a very long root (that's my excuse, anyway).

Unsurprisingly all the men who had scanner sex managed to achieve an orgasm but only half the women. Was it the missionary position or the huge noisy magnet that put them, off? We'll never know. Those who got there described the orgasm as 'superficial', whereas the women who went solo all achieved a good climax. This rather begs the question 'Are men really necessary (for orgasm in an MRI scanner)?' And as for the anatomical changes in women, the authors conclude that: 'During female sexual arousal the uterus was raised and the anterior vaginal wall lengthened, but the size of the uterus did not increase. '

So there. This study is one of a series of oddities that started back in 1933 with a man called Dickinson. He made a glass test

* Currently in The Royal Collection

tube in the shape of an erection and had good peek inside female subjects who were aroused by clitoral stimulation. Then came Masters and Johnson, who also used an artificial penis and 'direct observation.' They deduced that your uterus increases in size by up to 100% during arousal, a fact disputed by the Dutch study.

Perhaps the most extraordinary feature about this study has been the correspondence that has followed it. The *British Medical Journal* is not known for its agony column, but a retired chiropractor decided to write in and discuss his orgasmic difficulties following prostate surgery. Then there was a debate about whether the boomerang shape of the penis was down to the body scanner, rather than nature. In MRI scans, the body is placed inside a massive cylindrical magnet weighing 500 tons and subjecting the body to 60,000 times the earth's magnetic field. This excites the nuclei in the body's atoms which produce signals that can be recreated into pictures. Could such a force not bend a penis?

The answer is apparently not, unless the penis had something metal in it. Going into a huge magnet with a Prince Albert would be suicide. Then came a letter from an earnest American professor explaining why only half of the copulating women achieved orgasm:

> *The missionary position may be responsible.*
> *Human sexual anatomy seems to be designed for*
> *rear entry as practised by lower mammals where,*
> *presumably, greater stimulation of the anterior*
> *vaginal wall occurs and the semen is deposited*
> *closer to the cervical opening.*

Needless to say, this professor is male. An alternative explanation for the poor arousal rate came from a (female) colleague of mine.

> *MRI scanners are incredibly noisy and*
> *claustrophobic, you're not allowed to move and*

you know there's a load of boffins in the next room scrutinising your anatomy. Now some women might get off on that, but it's my idea of hell.

In fact, all the couples were willing volunteers and the researchers did their best to make them comfortable. As the *BMJ* article explains 'Participants were assured confidentiality, privacy, anonymity and the possibility of withdrawing from the study at any time . . .'

Is sex better for you if you do it outdoors?

It's not better for those watching, so always aim for somewhere remote. There's some evidence that being surrounded by nature is good for your mental health, but most people who have sex outdoors are trying to get it over with as quickly as possible, rather than taking time to smell the roses. If you're caught having sex so blatantly that it couldn't possibly be confused with searching for a contact lens, then in the UK you can be charged with indecent exposure in a public place (Town Police Clauses Act 1847). This could mean a £1,000 fine or, at worst, fourteen days in jail (though you'd need to be really going some up the Shed End). If you were genuinely looking for a contact lens and just got a bit carried away, you can still be done for breach of the peace though this is very noise dependant. As a rule, no more than one orgasm per contact lens. British police tend to be more lenient if they stumble across you by accident (unlucky on a remote grassy knoll) than if you've been shopped by humourless hikers. In Saudi Arabia, any public display of affection is outlawed and you'd be wise to pack a spare pair of contact lenses.

Things to do:

- **Keep as many clothes on as mechanically possible;**
- **Lie very still in the presence of Labradors;**
- **Call a time-out to remove twigs.**

Things not to do:

- **Try to fit two of you on a child's swing;**
- **Padlock yourself to railings in the dark;**
- **Find a nice spot covered in condoms and needles.**

Things to say when you're caught:

- **'Ah, there it is!'**
- **'Lovely evening, officer.'**
- **'Down, boy.'**

Things not to say when you're caught:

- **'Do you know who I am?'**
- **'Climb aboard, Jack, there's room on my horse for two.'**
- **'Here comes the money shot.'**

What's the best sex gadget on the market?

Most sex therapists say your imagination, closely followed by your tongue (or their own patented tongue extension or finger fiddler). I say, Fresh Drop poo odour remover (MOTTO: 'A fresh drop before you go and nobody will ever know'). The right setting is important for sex, particularly for women. You can clean the sheets and dim the lighting all you like but if you've just coiled off a code brown in the master en suite, there's no way she'll be in the mood until the pong's gone. One drop; that's all it takes. I don't have shares in this company, but I'm so impressed with it, I've plugged it twice. Once you've got rid of the smell, I recommend a generous smearing each of Dr Phil's Miracle Man Milk and Luscious Lady Lube (gift pack available).

Do Dr Phil's Miracle Man Milk and Luscious Lady Lube really exist?

No. If you need a lubricant that's easy to use (and won't destroy a condom), try Replens or Liquid Silk. KY Jelly is a bit gooey for my taste. Other condom-safe lubricants include egg whites, any water-based lubricants and good old-fashioned spit and saliva. Not terribly romantic but in the heat of the moment, drooling or gobbing on your partner's parts hits the spot for some folks. Lubricants to avoid if you want to withdraw with your condom/ relationship intact include baby oil, baby poo, body or hand lotion, massage oil, mineral oil, petroleum jelly, alcohol gel, suntan lotion, vegetable oil and Deep Heat (don't even think about it).

Do perpendicular penile piercings hurt?

I should imagine they do smart a bit to start with, yes. The magic cross is about as extreme as body piercing gets, involving both horizontal (ampallang) and front to back (apadravya) piercing of the glans (the bit that looks like a cherry). Whether it looks like a cherry after two metal rods are stuck through it is a moot point, but generally a magic cross takes about six months to heal, even in the best hands, before you can fully experience the pleasure of internal penis stimulation and your partner can enjoy those tiny metal dumb-bells rubbing up and down the uvula/vulva/G spot/ prostatic ridge/Ben and Jerry's Honeynut Crunch.

Do you favour open or closed swinging?

Most swinging ends in tears, either because some people are more up for it than others, some people thought they were up for it but really didn't enjoy it, and someone doesn't get picked at all (or, just as insulting, gets picked last). Bastards.

If I had to choose again, I'd probably go for closed swinging, where several couples meet together under the pretence of rehearsing for a village pantomime, and trade partners before returning to the person they came with. This at least gives you the reassurance of knowing roughly who you'll be playing with and, in theory, there should be no plump, white, ginger person prompting himself left of stage while everyone else is having fun. And if it all goes pear-shaped, you at least have someone familiar to moan to on the way home.

Open swinging is far more risky, because anyone could proposition you, including the anally retentive IT enthusiast, or everyone could ignore you, leaving you on your own in the corner playing Kerplunk. Which isn't that bad a game, as it happens . . . so long as you wear a condom.

What are the best party tricks to play with a very long penis?

You're asking the wrong person. However, I have been on enough rugby tours to see a pint mug filled to the brim with just one set of bollocks (it looked like a claustrophobic squid). And a long enough penis can poke through a hole in a front pocket and appear above the top edge: 'That's my spare one.' How we all laughed. For a dangly scrotum, you can bring a testicle right up, under the trouser line and then out over the belt line. It looks like a tense, angry and shockingly misplaced growth, but I'm not sure it's very good for your sperm count. And you can still be done for indecent exposure.

Do people really fall backwards whilst wallpapering the ceiling?

All the time. If someone's brave enough to come up to casualty with something stuck in their rectum, the least we can do is take their explanation at face value and with a straight face. One of the most important lessons I teach to medical students is how to hold it all together when a self-experimenter comes in. Laugh it off in the mess if you must, and keep a copy of the X-ray in your education folder, but we're here to help, not to judge.

Human development is fascinating. As we grow, we switch effortlessly from sticking things in our upper holes (mouth, nostrils, ears) to hiding them in our lower holes. Just as a big poo can give a pleasant sensation on the way out, so – apparently – can a solid object on the way in, particularly for men who have the added bonus of a prostate to stimulate. Butt-plugging is as old as the hills. In *Surgical Applied Anatomy* by Frederick Treves and Arthur Keith (published 1917), the authors recall removing a glass tumbler, a silver matchbox, a deer horn and an umbrella handle. Didn't they do well.

Take a wander (and wonder) round a medical school museum and you'll find an ancient 'foreign bodies' section, in between the kidney stones and the Elephant Man. As a student, I came across a pre-war door handle with the label attached: 'an unmarried man of forty-two admitted that the introduction of the handle was intended to produce an erotic sensation.' Such honesty should be rewarded. The most common response to delicate enquiries is, 'I don't want to talk about it', which is fair enough.

But the face-breaker is invariably when someone tries a fantastically implausible plausible explanation. In 1983, a *World Medicine* article by Dr Weston-Davies cited a man with a bottle of Heinz Tomato Ketchup in his rectum who claimed he'd lost his door keys and was climbing through the pantry window when he also lost his foothold. A brilliant alibi, and he might have got away with it had there not been a condom on the ketchup bottle. (**Note:** A condom on a ketchup bottle isn't a bad shout. It a) allows it to slip in more easily; b) prevents ketchup dispersal that is easily confused with rectal bleeding; and c) allows you to safely eat the ketchup, which we now know to be excellent for your prostate.)

Then there's the retired squadron leader who might actually have been telling the truth. He apparently used a Bofors anti-aircraft shell, circa 1945, to pop his prolapsed piles back in and he let go of the end in error. The surgeon summoned the bomb squad as well as the anaesthetist, and the patient escaped with shell shock.

The largest published collection of rectal foreign bodies (Drs Busch and Starling, *Surgery*, 1986) mercifully did not include any animals. There was the odd, rather obvious, 'vibrating abdomen syndrome' from a Duracell-powered toy. But top of the pops were glass or ceramics (fifty-six assorted jars, bottles, light bulbs and tubes, but not all from the same person). Fruit and veg were also popular (we tell you to take five portions a day, but not how to take them), as were wooden handles and body sprays ('Men can't help acting on Impulse'). My favourite category was 'miscellaneous', which included a tobacco pouch, a frozen pig's tail, a salami and an ice pick.

How do you remove a light bulb from the rectum?

You can't just wait for it to go out. First, you look at the X-ray to make sure it hasn't burst. Then you show the X-ray to a sweetly

naïve nursing student who says: 'How did he swallow a light bulb?'
(And it is nearly always a 'he.' I've never seen a woman with a
rectal foreign body that she put there herself. Women tend to use
properly designed butt-plugs on each other, which have a flared
end and so they can't disappear.)

Bailey and Love's *Short Practice of Surgery*, first published
seventy-five years ago, is the fount all knowledge:

> *The variety of foreign bodies that have found their*
> *way into the rectum is hardly less remarkable*
> *than the ingenuity displayed in their removal. A*
> *turnip has been removed per annum by the use of*
> *obstetric forceps. A stick firmly impacted has been*
> *withdrawn inserting a gimlet into its lower end.*
> *A tumbler, mouth looking downwards, has been*
> *extracted by filling the interior with a wet plaster*
> *of Paris bandage . . .*

It makes you wish *What's My Line?* was still on the telly.

Low-watt bulbs are better for the environment but not for
your bowel, on account of the complex shape. The only technique
I've come across is to cover it in strips of papier mâché, allow
them to set, break the bulb and gently withdraw with plenty of
lube. Failing that, it's a scalpel.

Who owns the X-ray?

Technically it's the hospital, but you could offer to pay for a copy.
You could also ask for it not to appear in a review of the world's
literature or the *Sunday Times* colour supplement. Anuses may
be as loose as ever, but the rules on patient confidentiality have
tightened up over the years. In the old days, doctors could merrily

take your X-rays and hilarious anecdotes around the conference, after-dinner and daytime-TV circuits, without your permission. The only rule was that individuals couldn't be identified. Unlikely, as one light bulb in the rectum looks much the same as another.

These days, the General Medical Council and all reputable medical journals like you to get written consent to use stories or photos from living patients, even if they can't be identified. This has rather laid waste to the publication of rectal foreign body round-ups in the press. 'Hello Mr Jones, Dr Hammond here. Remember that time when you lost your keys and you were climbing in through the pantry window? Yes, well, I'm filling in for Dr Hilary on GMTV and I wondered if . . . ?' A few brave after-dinner medics are still doing the rounds, and often protect themselves by anecdote-swapping (claiming things that happened to colleagues, happened to them and vice versa). And in any case, when you're half-way through the great tobacco pouch mystery, it's very rare for someone to put his hand up and shout: 'Hey, that's me, that is!'

Is it possible to whip someone in the context of a loving relationship?

Yes, but only after they've taken the rubbish out. If you've been together for a few years or more and the sex routine has become as mechanical as the toddler/dog/recycling routine, it's not easy to suggest something a bit off-piste. Which I guess is why people pay to be whipped by strangers. However, it's a lot cheaper (and less likely to end up in the tabloids) if you can encourage your partner to do it. If it's a desire you've been hiding for many years, it's really hard to just come out with it. Communication experts recommend the old third-person ploy: 'I bumped into Bob the other day, Hadn't seen him for years. He really enjoys being whipped.' 'Have you taken the rubbish out?' Works every time. Failing that, drop 'whipme' into Sex Scrabble.

How do I tell if my partner is dominant, submissive or not interested?

It's probably best to ask. Some people who are dominant in the day job (politicians, judges, doctors, priests, teachers, referees) like to dress up in nappies and be humiliated in private. Psychoanalysts have had a field day postulating why an individual might get into sexual domination and submission, and how it differs from assault. According to sex therapist William Henkin, a lot of couples get involved in power struggles, where each tries to control the other without ever resolving the problems. S&M provides a safe and consensual environment to work through these issues.

Some theorists claim a liking for S&M is all in the genes, others go for the 'something in childhood playing out in later life' theme; a bearded nanny, a sadistic teacher, an over-protective mother or holidays on the farm. There is no evidence I can find that those who practise consensual kinky sex are any more likely to have been abused as children than those who stick to two minutes of hide the sausage and a good book. Neither do they seem to have been damaged or destroyed by any other traumatic event. They just enjoy the feeling of buttock on willow. And vice versa.

None of this is new. Water sports (golden showers, urophilia, whatever) date back to Ancient Egypt and were common in the court of Louis IV. Fellatio on park benches overlooking the Serpentine is very common in nineteenth-century photos, but you'd struggle to get away with it today (**TIP**: Use the picnic blanket). Anything you could possibly imagine (and plenty you can't) can be found on an ancient Japanese woodcut or in a French cartoon. And what's the Cerne Abbas Giant doing with a huge erection and a knobbly club in his hand?

For 5,000 years, every society has realised that controlling sexual relationships is the best way to discipline people, and there have always been people prepared to challenge that view. The tighter the morals, the wider the rebellion. In Victorian England, when men were supposed to limit their animal desires to once a month and never during pregnancy or periods, prostitution, flagellation, boy brothels and S&M pornography were popular, and the dressing ring was born – a metal hoop inserted through the glans to increase sexual stimulation and secure the penis to the leg of the trousers when dressing; also known as a 'Prince Albert.' But it wasn't all fun, fun, fun. Syphilis killed thousands. Condom, condom, condom . . .

My granny used to say: 'Pleasure is a two-way street but your anus doesn't have to be.' Was she right?

Right again. In any one year, around twelve per cent of men and eleven per cent of women try anal sex, if only the once, and nearly ninety per cent manage to avoid it.

If you're considering taking the plunge, the crucial starting point as with all sex is consent, and preferably even desire. If you don't want to stick your penis in an anus, or be on the receiving end, then it's unlikely to be a success. And never spring it on an unwitting partner with the old 'Whoops, sorry, wrong hole!' line.

If you both agree to give it a go, you should approach it with the same caution you would if you were driving the wrong way up a one-way street, in the dark . . . and blindfolded. It's not uncommon to meet traffic coming the other way at great speed so put an old towel down and be prepared to bail out. If you haven't dropped the kids off at the pool that day, you're probably courting disaster.

If you have a lot of anal sex (or just once very roughly), then the sphincter can be damaged and the anus loses its ability to tell what's passing through. So be gentle. Here's what you need:

- Mutual consent and desire
- Time
- A time-out sign
- Empty-ish bowel
- An old towel
- Lubrication (lots of it and not the condom-dissolving kind)
- Finger first (just the one)
- A dental dam (for rimming or root canal work)
- A very firm put preferably not too huge erection (anything remotely soft won't work)
- A condom (preferably extra strength)
- More lubrication
- A tentative nudge followed by a slow and gentle stroke
- A Plan B
- A sense of humour

How anyone manages such a technical procedure on a windswept common in the dark with a dark stranger is quite beyond me. The absolute minimum is a condom. Without one, it's more likely to hurt, more likely to pass on infection (particularly hepatitis, gonorrhoea and HIV) and more likely that one of you will end up with a tide mark or corn on the cob. Some women say they enjoy a pleasant feeling of rectal fullness, some frankly don't. Men get the double-whammy of rectal fullness and prostate stimulation.

The abundance of strap-on toys allows heterosexual couples to do some adventurous role-reversal (known humorously as 'pegging'). The same rules apply but if you get the giggles, the sphincter will tighten and you probably won't get anywhere near penetration. At least he'll realise the intimate joy of kneeling with arse in the air and face asphyxiated in a pillow.

GAMES VERY FEW PEOPLE PLAY

Is docking possible without a foreskin?

Docking means different things in different contexts. Mooring your boat, arranging a space rendezvous, or having your dog's tail trimmed should not be confused with its more modern interpretation (placing the glans of your penis into the foreskin on someone else's). You could combine the two, I suppose, but you'd need to find a fairly liberated vet. Clearly, if you have no foreskin, you can only be the donor and not the recipient. It also helps if you're on at least nodding acquaintance with your fellow dockers.

Does teabagging taste better with sugar?

Teabagging has yet to make it into the Scrabble Dictionary, but it surely won't be long after its appearance in *The Australian*, the country's premier broadsheet. On August 27, 2009, legal affairs correspondent Michael Pelly reported:

> *Australia's supreme military disciplinary body has been ruled illegal by the High Court in a decision that has thrown military justice into turmoil. The government has been forced to rewrite the military justice system after the High Court blocked the prosecution of a leading seaman charged with indecent assault for placing his genitals on a sleeping colleague's forehead – a practice known as 'teabagging'.*

The allegations were in any case refuted ('There was no teabagging at Roma's Motel, Carnarvon. Skylarking, yes. Teabagging, no.') and there's absolutely no reason why you shouldn't sign up either to the Australian Navy or visit what appears to be a very pleasant motel (www.motelcarnarvon.com.au/). Even better, when your partner lays down a paltry 'tea' during knackered Scrabble, think where your bingo bagging could lead? (A bingo is a seven-letter get out that earns an extra fifty on top of your teabagging).

Teabagging is not to everyone's taste, although a sugary scrotum could make it marginally more palatable. The angle of the dangle is critical for success. Teabagging is safest with the recipient upright, when there is less risk of asphyxiation and more opportunity for escape. You can either close your eyes and hope it goes away, or open your mouth and hope for the best. It's always worth asking before taking a whole testicle (and certainly two) in your mouth, as some men are more sensitive (and nervous) than others.

Horizontal teabagging is another experience entirely, as the testicles abseil down from above and can land pretty much anywhere. Dominant partners are more likely to dangle onto submissive ones, and if you both enjoy the erotic humiliation then fine. But consent is the key and it's always worth having a get out clause. Teabagging for the over-sixties is easier in one sense (things dangle down more) but looks even more inelegant and there's always the danger that your hips will give way and you'll topple down into a full-on squat.

Teabagging has been used for centuries as an initiation rite into assorted male groups, but received wider recognition thanks to a fleeting appearance in the 1998 John Waters film *Pecker*. If you're thinking of trying it, Dr Phil's formula for the perfect teabagging is as follows:

$$Tb = \frac{C^1 \times C^2 \times V \times L \times H}{T \times F \times S \times M \times I}$$

Where C^1 and C^2 are the recipient's level of consciousness and consent, V is degree of verticality and L is lung capacity. H represents the hip stability of the donor. The denominators are quantitative measures of the donor's thrust and frequency of dunking, scent, moulting and inappropriate commentary. Enjoy!

Have you ever seen bladder tennis go to five sets?

No. Bladder tennis is played almost exclusively in London medical schools. Two people (generally male and of an ex-public school, rugby-playing persuasion) catheterise each other, join the catheters up in the middle and then score a point for each time they manage to pee into their opponent's bladder. The game presents a number of logistic challenges. The act of catheterisation removes sphincter control from the bladder so it's hard to shoot with any force, especially from behind the baseline. Also, it's a very hard game to score. With no umpire or hawk-eye, there is no satisfactory way of resolving disputed line calls. Finally, unlike Wimbledon, the gladiators are generally so drunk that I've never seen a game advance beyond 30–15 before rain stops play.

Can you make your own Sailors' Sweetheart?

Yes. It's generally not something you'll see on *Blue Peter*, but a lot of men get through hard times by fashioning their own penile repository. A sock or an oven-glove allows you to fantasise about a hirsute hand job. Soft fruits are a safe favourite, not least because they have enough give in them to allow for expansion (**TIP**: Wait until you've got back from the grocers). Avoid the neck of a milk bottle; although it scores well for friction, the thrusting action creates a vacuum, rather like the pump-action cork in a wine bottle. This can cause a really rather impressive expansion but no way of relief without a trip to casualty.

Is it legal to keep 2p pieces in your foreskin?

Yes, but not terribly community-spirited. Some men have remarkably long and prehensile foreskins, and I have seen a medical student (now a consultant orthopaedic surgeon) unfurl the foreskin as if taking the rubber sleeve off a cricket bat, stack twenty-two old 10ps on top of the glands, retract the skin and stand up, leaving this loose change dangling without support and cleverly hidden from pickpockets. I suspect this is only illegal if you leave one behind and it stays there so long that the Queen is defaced. It will also make you pee all over the floor even more.

What's the best shoe for playing freckle?

Freckle is best not played at all. If you must, do so at the end of the evening, after bladder tennis but while the bar is nearly empty but still open. It's a game of staggering simplicity. Players gather around a table with a pack of cards which are dealt sequentially, face up. The first person to get an ace has to defecate in the centre of the table. The second person to be dealt an ace has to take his shoe off and bring it down with full force onto the turd. The person who ends up with the most freckles, has to buy the next round.

In cases of dispute (generally when one or more players have freckles to start with), it's wise to take a pre-game photo on the mobile to judge which spots are natural and which are late additions. A randomised controlled trial comparing different shoes has failed to attract sufficient funding but generally, stilettos give disappointing results. The best coverage I've witnessed has been from a fourteen-hole cherry red Dr Martin (right boot, air-ware, not cushion sole).

NOTE: It's important to get people to sign a public health disclaimer before attempting this game.

Do people really put hamsters up there?

Lots of people pretend to do it on YouTube (perhaps it accounts for Gordon Brown's peculiarly unnatural grin) but none of the films I've looked at contain a money shot. I fear it's at least been attempted somewhere. Humans have a seemingly exhaustible appetite for experimentation, self-indulgence and animal cruelty. And hamsters have great difficulty saying 'no'. Placing a large piece of cheese or an exercise-wheel up there first does not constitute informed consent.

I have found a discussion board suggesting the use of a cardboard tube as a runway, and a rodent with a bushy tail so you can fish it out again. But in an exhaustive search of the medical literature, I've found no evidence of anyone seeking medical help for a secretly concealed cricetinus. Of far more interest, at least to *Countdown* viewers, is that fact that most of the population pronounces 'hamster' as 'hampster.' There is no 'p' in hamster; particularly if it's dehydrated and half-way up your ascending colon.

Is it true they make plaster casts of your penis when you're under anaesthetic?

Only if you've given your consent and paid for the handling. It's far easier buy a penis moulding kit online and fashion your own spare (with balls attached) in latex, rubber or silicone and a choice of six colours and eighteen flavours. And if you squeeze the balls before they set, you can add on a few inches for good measure. Now you just have to find someone to give it to.

Can you swaddle a penis?

Yes. The ancient art of swaddling involves wrapping your penis in cloth or cotton wool to double its girth before hiding it in a condom. The glans at the end is generally left uncovered, to allow some sensation, and the swaddling is secured with rubber bands. Even if you do manage to get away with this ridiculous sleight of penis, there's always a chance that the condom will slip off, particularly at the end when everything shrinks down. You then have some explaining to do: 'I wanted to keep the heat in so I lagged it' might just pass muster. If you're really brave, you can wrap it in layers and dispense with the condom altogether, offering it to the group as a game of Pass the Parcel, where the final prize isn't quite as big as expected, but everyone's too polite to say so.

Where can I ride a human pony?

At home. All you need is a willing partner with a strong back. The bridal harness is optional, and so is the sex *(coitus à cheval)*. If you want to see how it's done, check out the website of Danny the Wonder Pony. www.wonderpony.com As Danny puts it:

> *I get down on all fours and the lady sits in the saddle. Her feet go in the stirrups and I stand up and dance . . . Because I'm not shaped like a horse, I've studied and developed moves that correlate with a pony.*

Women find this stimulating, Danny thinks, because being on a pony was often their first sexual experience.

> *Western saddles are better than English ones*
> *– they've got a horn and a slope at the front*
> *... Having women jump on my back isn't*
> *unpleasurable but I really have to put forth effort.*

Does he get turned on? 'Well, sure, mentally, in the same way as a weightlifter. You're concentrating on lifting 300lbs, not getting an erection.' So now you know. You can either buy back your old pony, fly to New York and hire Danny for the evening, or tempt your partner into the show ring. Or you could just fantasise about those golden Pony Club days. It may not give you the same adrenaline rush as the real thing, but there's no mucking out and you'll save a fortune on osteopathy bills.

Can you catheterise yourself with tubular pasta?

No. If you insist on trying (and I'm assuming only a man would), you need to cook it until it's *al dente*. Then wash your hands thoroughly, retract the foreskin (if applicable) and stretch the penis perpendicular to the body to eliminate any urethral folds that may lead to false passage. Steady gentle pressure should be used to advance the pasta-catheter, and any significant obstruction encountered should prompt withdrawal and re-insertion. Insert the pasta to the hilt and wait till urine emerges before blowing in the end to create a balloon. Remember to reposition the foreskin to prevent massive oedema of the glans.

NOTE: This is a ridiculous and foolhardy hobby, and a shameful waste of pasta.

Is it possible to have a phobia of penis-like musical instruments?

It's possible to have a phobia about anything. This one goes by the name of 'aulophobia' and you may need to change your music teacher.

Yeah, right. And I suppose there's a name for getting off on ants crawling all over your genitals?

Yep, that one's 'formicophilia'. It's generally includes all small insects and snails.

Getting turned on by watching a loved one having sex with an animal?

'Mixoscopia bestialis.' The fact that sexologists have given it a label seems to confer an acceptability that probably shouldn't be there.

Sniffing women's shoes?

That's more like it. 'Retifism'.

7

About Dr Phil

Dr Phil is a part time GP and comedian, who's also worked in sexual health. He writes regularly for the *Mendip Times* and hides regularly in the Mendips. He appears in every *Private Eye* and occasionally on *Countdown, Have I Got News For You, The News Quiz, The Now Show, The Gabby Logan Show, The Music Group* and *Radio Bristol*. He is a patron of the Herpes Viruses Association and a Vice President of the Patients Association. His greatest pleasure is pretending to be somewhere else.

What's your favourite sexual move?

I love the word 'frottage' but no doctor can condone arousal by rubbing up against strangers in a crowded casualty department. Apparently, this is a paraphilia of the solicitational-allurative type, as well as a good way to start a fight, and the perpetrator is known as a 'frotteur' (or a filthy bastard, depending on which school you went to).

I also like the sound of 'bundling', a colonial American courtship custom where couples slept together allegedly to conserve heat and eliminate the need for the man to ride home in the dark. Premarital sex was discouraged by enclosing the woman up to her armpits in a bundling bag. It wasn't very successful, particularly after the invention of scissors,

Bundling sounds preferable to 'fenstern' ('window courting'), a German custom to ensure all wives produced farm-workers. Women keen on marriage hung a lantern in their bedroom window, with a ladder up to it. Young men did the rounds but left before dawn. Women who subsequently got pregnant could choose any one of the visitors as their husband, not necessarily the father. In Scandinavia, a similar custom is known as 'taking your night feet for a walk' and the Mangaians of the South Pacific call it 'motoro' or night crawling. To me it smacks a bit of 'droit de seigneur'; the 'right' of a medieval lord to deflower the bride of any serf. Also known as 'jus primae noctis' ('the right of the first night'). **TIP:** Find out what 'Bugger off, my Lord' is in Latin.

How much do you drink?

Like any drug, I take the smallest dose that does the trick. My current medication is a bottle of Coopers Brewery Pale Ale (Australian Made, Australian Owned) a night. It's only 4.5 per cent but it tastes great and it uses 'a centuries old top fermentation method and natural bottle conditioning, resulting in a characteristic fine sediment' – which keeps my bowels silky smooth and regular.

What's the rudest thing you learnt at medical school?

I learnt some shocking games, detailed above for reference purposes only. Over twenty years later, the rude mnemonics still stick. For example, there are five branches of the facial nerve which I've just had to look up because I can't remember them (temporal, zygomatic, buccal, mandibular and cervical). However, I can clearly recall the mnemonic I was taught at St Thomas's: 'Two Zulus buggered my cat.' A friend at Guys used a slight variation: 'Two Zulus bit my cock.' Does it matter? I suppose it does if you're a Zulu. And in the heat of your finals viva, you only remember the mnemonic. 'What's the fifth branch of the facial nerve?' 'Cat . . . Sorry, I meant cock.'

Even though apartheid was in full swing, this mnemonic is the only context that Zulus were mentioned in my six years at medical school, apart from the song about Zulu warriors, which we sang with trousers down in the bar. But I don't recall this as a protest against forced segregation. Medical school was a conformist cocoon, and we rarely challenged abuses of power in medicine, let alone the wider world. However, I did recently ask a medical student what today's mnemonic is for the branches of the facial nerve. 'Two zebras buggered my cat.' Whatever happened to animal rights?

Have you ever been reported to the GMC?

Only once that I know of (but there could be a few complaints piling up in the in-tray), and it was for the piece below I wrote for the *Daily Express* on 25 June 1998.

> *As a doctor, people often ask me 'Is William Hague being a wimp?' This seems a desperately uncharitable thing to say about the leader of Her Majesty's Opposition, but he has been off with flu for six days now. It started, rather ominously, on the anniversary of his succession to the leadership, amid backbench rumours that Fat Ken is plotting his downfall. He then pulled out of the vote to lower the age of homosexual sex and cancelled a lecture he was due to give under catchy title 'local*

institutions'. Not even Prime Minister's Questions could tempt him back from his sick bed. We're used to Party Leaders looking a little peaky – John Major looked permanently shattered towards the end of his tortuous reign and success has hardly been kind to Tony Blair – but we expect them to soldier on against the odds. When Thatcher had surgery for her Dupuytren's contracture (curvature of the fingers) she was back at work the same day. Hague gets the sniffles and he's on his back for a week.

To be fair, flu is far more than the sniffles. The influenza virus can floor even the most sprightly politician, and Hague needs to get his rest in now if he's to avoid fatigue later. A week is the average recovery time and if he needs more, he'll have to bring in a doctor's note for Miss Boothroyd. I'm sure she'll understand. In the caring nineties, it's fine for would-be world leaders to acknowledge their viral susceptibility. If that's what it is. June isn't the commonest time to get flu and I haven't seen any other sufferers, but with the amount of meeting and greeting he does, he could easily pick up any number of bugs. Susceptibility to viral illnesses depends in part on your mental state. Happy in-control people tend to avoid them, while the persecuted and over-worked drop like flies. Is Mr Hague's body trying to tell him something?

That same day, I was sent letter by William Hague's press secretary:

Dear Dr Hammond

I read your article in today's Daily Express. I was surprised that a doctor would wish to put himself out on a limb like this by offering a medical opinion on an individual you have never seen and have no knowledge about. It is no surprise, therefore, that your article was inaccurate and worse it was insulting. For your information, Mr Hague has had a bout of flu complicated by acute sinusitis – as a doctor you should surely be aware of the pain this can cause.

I thought the article was highly unprofessional and a poor advert for your profession. I have copied this letter to your editor and to the General Medical Council for their information.

Yours Sincerely
Gregor Mackay

A few weeks later, I got a very sweet letter from the GMC saying they had looked into the matter but as I wasn't, and had never been, William Hague's doctor, there had been no breach of confidentiality and my speculations were not a matter for them.

In December 2005, I met Bob 'the Cat' Bevan, an after-dinner speaker of some repute who also writes the odd gag for William Hague. He'd met Gregor Mackay and was amazed at his letter because he was so charming and charismatic. But then politics makes you behave in peculiar ways.

On the way home, I borrowed a copy of *The Times* from first class and it carried Mackay's obituary. Dead at thirty-six from non-Hodgkin's lymphoma. For someone I'd never met and had very little knowledge about, I was surprisingly upset. He was joint Scottish schoolboy doubles tennis champion for two successive years. 'While professional in his work, he was always able to find something to laugh at, even during the darkest days of the Tory meltdown of 1997.' I wish I'd had a beer with him now. And his memorial fund helps treat cancer patients at the hospital where I trained. Why not join me in a donation?

www.gsttcharity.org.uk/fundraising/gregormackay-memorialfund.html

Have you ever missed a pregnancy?

Yes. In my defence, the one diagnosis I was taught not to miss was depression, and the woman in question had insomnia, headache, fatigue, backache and changeable mood, all of which are common symptoms of depression. Alas, they're also common symptoms of pregnancy. And, of course, you can be pregnant and depressed. It's not easy making the right diagnosis first time, every time, which I guess is why doctors have an exalted position in society (until we get something wrong, and are hung out to dry with the bankers and MPs). I've only knowingly made the mistake once and I now ask all women, from seven to seventy, if they might be pregnant, whatever their symptoms.

Have you ever put anything smaller than your elbow in your ear?

Yes. I used to do that thing with cotton buds until the end of one came off, like they always warn you, and I was so embarrassed that I tried to get it out myself with various rusty old tools I had from my dissecting kit when I was a medical student (these are the tools that had previously been used to dissect dead flesh, but I did give them a wash.) When that didn't work, I tried to flush it out with a high pressure shower head. I couldn't tell whether that had worked so I rather reluctantly asked my wife, Dr Rose, to check if she could see anything abnormal in my ear. 'Why?' 'No particular reason.'

She spotted a white bit, wasn't sure what it was, couldn't

shift it and – as we were about to go on holiday – insisted I had someone look at it. I wasn't sure I could face the accident and emergency department, joining the queue of other children with beads in their ears/nostrils/windpipe. So I emailed a friendly ENT consultant who agreed to see me without having to parade my stupidity in front of assorted receptionists, nurses and junior doctors (who I'd probably taught at some stage).

> '**There's no cotton bud in your ear?**'
> '**So what's the white thing my wife can see?**'
> '**An exostosis.**'
> '**Will I find it on Wikipedia?**'
> '**It's a bit of bone that often grows in the ears of surfers and swimmers to protect the drum from the rush of cold water.**'
> '**Do I need it removed?**'
> '**Can you hear alright?**'
> '**Yes.**'
> '**No then. Just don't put anything else in your ear.**'
> '**Are you sure it's not a pebble?**'
> '**Yes. Why do you ask?**'

Back in 1987, I was a medical student, on an elective in India with my friend Sube (who's now a Professor of Psychiatry). This was a period of study meant to give us experience of how the health service worked abroad. Most students took it terribly seriously, some even picking up scalpels and whipping out appendices in remote huts in faraway countries with no lawyers. Sube and I weren't interested in such heroics. We just wanted to slob out on the beach before our final exams and the drudgery of house-jobs.

We did visit one hospital, in Calcutta, and were amazed at the diagnostic ability of a doctor who had no access to machines to do the thinking for you. He just sat and listened. When he fell through the rotting floor of the hospital, we decided we'd seen enough listening and travelled across to Delhi, through Rajasthan, down to Mumbai and on to Goa.

I'd like to tell you about the lavish temples, colourful festivals and the potent architectural relics of Old Goa, but we didn't move much from the sea. When we arrived, we rented a hut on the nearest beach. It had a top of the range 'pig system toilet'. You shat through a hole in the floor and the pigs ate it. Alas, we didn't spot this revelatory method of sanitation until our third night of spaghetti carbonara (and surprisingly tasty it was too).

For sterilisation, we discovered feni, a potent spirit allegedly distilled from cashew fruit but with bits floating in it. Too much could turn you blind – the high ethanol content takes out the optic nerve – and alarms bells should have rung when the feni man appeared with a very low budget guide dog (more of a pig, to be fair).

We were sitting on the beach in a post-feni blur, when a boy approached us and asked if we'd like to have our ears checked for the stones which get stuck after swimming. Sube sensibly declined and carried on reading his Freud. But I didn't like the idea of swimmers' stones in my ear, so I let him look. He discovered four in each ear, calling on Sube to witness them. He then quoted me a lump sum, roughly equivalent to all my remaining rupees, fished the stones out with a pair of long-toothed tweezers and left a lot richer.

For a few days I was convinced my hearing was better, so I shared my story with the blind feni-man, who I thought could do with some tips on preserving his hearing.

'Doh! He put the stones in there to take them out again, you gullible ginger tit.'

'How did you know I was ginger?'

I learnt a lot from this. Doctors are human and we don't always follow our own advice, especially under the hot sun in a strange country after a couple of fenis. But there's no excuse for experimenting with cotton buds in the privacy of your own bathroom. You only push the wax in further, when it backs up against the exostosis and you can't hear a bloody thing. No more neighbour's car alarm, no more children fighting, no more being asked to put the rubbish out. Bliss, in fact.

What's the biggest wobbly a patient's thrown in front of you?

When I worked in casualty, a boy came in who'd spent ages collecting small objects for his school 'how many things can you fit in a matchbox?' competition. He'd been brilliantly inventive (a milk tooth, a staple, a bogey, a pubic hair, a woodlouse, a cat biscuit, a drawing pin, something that might be a chocolate raisin but we're not sure, the tail of a rodent that the cat had left by the back door etc etc). On the day of judging, he left his prize collection by the front door so he wouldn't forget it. His toddler brother spied it, opened the box and wolfed the lot, pretty much down in one.

Cue three hysterical people in reception. Toddler didn't like the after taste and Mum thought he was going to die. But his brother was so upset, he could have been auditioning for Golem. 'Make him sick! Make him sick! Give me my precious things.' Triage that. We observed the toddler for a while and he was fine. The human digestive system has an amazing capacity to absorb punishment. But the brother was scarred for life.

Have you ever tried anything illicit?

I had a fairly routine, curious youth until I discovered that whatever gets you through the night stops you functioning during the day. And you don't need any form of stimulant to wonder at an orchid that mimics the sexual parts of a bee. There's so much joy and fascination out there in the everyday that it doesn't need expanding or mellowing. And it's quite possible to dance without ten bottles of Sol and some horse anaesthetic.

Have you ever tested legal drugs?

Yes, as a medical student I did quite a few 'first in human' trials, not out of altruism but because I needed the money. The Guy's hospital unit took pretty much anyone who wasn't diseased, pregnant or a Guy's student (very embarrassing to kill one of your own), and whose liver didn't extend much further than the navel. Some trials were residential, some had me cycling from Lambeth to London Bridge with a twenty-four-hour urine collection balanced on the handlebars (far riskier than any of the drugs I took).

Lots of students refused to do trials in a 'you must be stupid, you don't know what you're taking' sort of way. Others only went for trials of new batches of established drugs, but I was game for anything. I can't remember the name of a single drug I tested, but at £500 for a lost weekend it kept the bank manager happy. The only drawback was that the multiple needle holes marked you out like any other user.

If you were lucky, you got a placebo. Only once did anything really bad happen. A bloke in front of me in the queue had an anaphylactic reaction. Presumably that wasn't placebo. We all just stood there as he was resuscitated, trying to remember the correct dose of adrenaline and mulling over how much we really needed the £500. None of us walked out.

The staff were relatively easy to humour, although they did all have beards and kept us under lock and key. One made the mistake of letting a student out to bulk buy MacDonalds, or at least the bits of MacDonalds that don't affect your liver enzymes. He left the door ajar to allow several conscripts to sneak out to the pub over the road. They were guilty of scientific fraud, but seventy-two hours is an awfully long time to make a medical student go without beer. Sadly, the unit's director spotted the bum pressed up against the pub window and docked it £200, which was a lot of money in those days but nothing compared to the drug company who finds its new wonder drug does unexpectedly horrible things to the liver.

Generally, people do well in drug trials, especially further down the line when they've figured out how safe it is and how much to give. And in the NHS, it may be the only way to get an expensive new drug. Even if you get a placebo or the standard treatment, you get far more attention than normal because people are desperate for you to do well. Tea, coffee, nurses that smile, foot massages. Stapled to my donor card, I've put a PS. 'In the event of me being unconscious, please enter me in a drug trial. If that fails, let me die quickly and take anything you need.'

Have you ever had a TUBE?

Totally Unnecessary Breast Examinations are rare in men but I've had one, while walking from New Street Station in Birmingham to the British Renal Society conference at the ICC on Broad Street. I was pulling a wheely-bag at the time, and off guard, when a bloke just walked up and grabbed by moobs. It wasn't painful but it threw me a bit, like a good heckle. Last time I was at the ICC, a bloke ran very fast across the atrium towards me and said: 'I know you. You're Lenny Henry.' He then kissed me and ran off. There's something about Birmingham. More parks than Paris, more canals than Venice and very friendly perverts.

Have you ever been whipped?

Yes. It wasn't, alas, a private exchange of power for pleasure amongst two consenting adults but a very public and painful flogging at the end of my stag party. I'd gained the prior consent of my best man that no 'o-grams' of any sort would be deployed, but another friend made a spur of the moment judgement on a card in a phone kiosk and, an hour later, in strode a terse woman in a black PVC bodysuit, six-inch spiked heeled leather boots and a cat o' nine tails. She was at the end of a bad evening and took her venom out on my rump. Although I'd had the equivalent of a general anaesthetic's worth of lager, the pain was extraordinary. My yelps were apparently much funnier than any joke I've ever told. And the lash marks were still with me on the wedding night. Lights off and under the duvet, quick. 'Why are you sleeping with your boxer shorts on?' 'Am I?'

For some reason, being degraded in a French restaurant by a stranger on your stag night is a cultural norm, whereas doing it for fun with your soulmate in the privacy of your home dungeon is considered taboo. But maybe that's what makes it exciting. Transgressing the borders of the forbidden, and all that. My local subdom club, the Stowey Bottom Users Group, suggests a couple of books on the subject if you fancy giving it a go. *The Loving Dominant* by John and Libby Warren (written in an amusing style for dominants and submissives, and with a handy chapter on first aid), and *Screw the Roses, Send Me the Thorns* by Philip Miller and Molly Devon (featuring knots, rope harnesses, making your own equipment, correct flogging methods and a thorough anatomy lesson with target areas and places to avoid clearly marked). And remember you are allowed to laugh uncontrollably, an entirely natural reaction to being shackled to the mattress handles with the Maypole ribbons. Trust me.

Have you ever had a dose?

Yes. Gonorrhoea, just the once, nearly thirty years ago. But I still remember the pus; rivers of the stuff, right through my boxer shorts and into my theatre greens. In my defence, people of my age (forty-seven) often kicked off their sexual careers before HIV arrived, and we weren't as careful as we should have been. Plus the fact that when you've got ginger hair, freckles and glasses, you're so amazed that someone will have sex with you, precautions go out of the window (or at least remain in the back pocket of the jeans on the other side of the room).

The consultant at Westminster hospital didn't have to put anything down my penis because it was dripping out. He got so excited, he invited me backstage to peer down the microscope: 'Look at that! Gram negative intracellular diplococci. Aren't they beautiful?' Not as beautiful as a condom, matey. To cheer me up, he told me about all the film stars, MPs, judges and clergy he'd treated in the clinic.

We're all susceptible to pleasure. I once chaired a conference of sexual health consultants and asked them to put their hand up (in the air) if they'd knowingly had at least one sexually transmitted infection. Six did. Then I asked the same question via the confidential conference keypad. 106 had; well over half the room. It's one of the few specialties where the doctors treating you know what they're talking about.

What would you like to be if you weren't a doctor?

An Honorary Lecturer in Applied Pleasure in the Department of Modified Hedonism at Mendip University, Stowey Bottom.

Do you still have your penis enlarger?

Yes. I grow cacti in it.

Do patients take you seriously?

Occasionally. And I can be terribly serious when I have to be.

Have you ever been anyone's wonder pony?

Not yet. But I live in hope.

What are your favourite Sex Scrabble words?

The beauty of Sex Scrabble is that it's part game, part foreplay, part therapy, and allows you to get issues and desires out there that you're too shy to drop into general chat. Slang aside, the sex literature is littered with ridiculously long and convoluted words of more than seven letters. For challenges, I recommend *The Complete Dictionary of Sexology (New Expanded Edition)*. It's quite hard to get hold of, so here are a few of my favourites:

acrai — Arabic term for a woman who really enjoys her sex.

amourette — a short-term affair in French, and an extension of amour.

ampulla — the opening of a tube, e.g. fallopian.

analist — a person whose erotic fantasies are focused on the anus. Easily confused with analyst. From spreadsheets to spreadcheeks.

balanic — pertaining to the glans of the penis or clitoris.

blissom — a blissful state of sexual heat.

bowser — a merkin.

carezza (or karezza) – Tantric intercourse in which erection and insertion are prolonged by minimal thrusting and without ejaculation. Note: don't rely on this for contraception.

copulin – a vaginal pheromone first isolated from a rhesus monkey that encourages the male to copulate.

dasypygal – having hairy buttocks (and worth stealing 2 extra letters for).

eonism – transvestism.

frenum – very sensitive part of the penis just below the glans on the underside. Some people pierce it for pleasure.

guiche – a metal ring inserted in the perineum, twixt genitals and anus, and pulled on lightly for pleasure. Not to be confused with quiche.

herm – a stone sculpture popular in ancient Greece with the head of Hermes and a large phallus at the base. More a symbol of male power than a celebration of sex.

kimilue – a triad of extreme apathy, loss of interest in life and vivid sexual dreams found among the Diegueno Indians of lower California and most teenage boys.

koro – a morbid fear of shrinking genitals brought on by masturbatory guilt or promiscuity. In some Eastern cultures, a wise Aunt is wheeled out to prevent reabsorption.

mahu – the sole transvestite in Polynesian villages who allows otherwise heterosexual men a casual outlet.

nonage – someone below the legal age for whatever you happen to be discussing.

olisbis – a leather phallus used in lesbian sex.

onanism – masturbation or withdrawal before climax, named after the biblical character Onan who was punished for spilling his seed on the ground.

orchis – Greek for testicle, based on the observation that the flower of the Lady Slipper orchid looks like a scrotum. Now why would God do that?

passion – an extreme, compelling emotion, drive or excitement. Vital for life but it needn't have anything to do with sex.

philia – non sexual love shared by friends.

spac – small penis anxiety complex. Vanishingly rare.

ALSO BY DR PHIL

Medicine Balls – a self help medical comedy with poems
Trust Me, I'm (Still) a Doctor – shocking secrets of an NHS
whistleblower

FURTHER BROWSING

www.embarrassingproblems.com

www.idler.co.uk

www.drphil2.com